TITLE II

Developing a Superior
Football-Control Attack

Developing a Superior Football-Control Attack

Vincent
J.
Dooley

Parker Publishing Company, Inc.

West Nyack, New York

PRINTED IN THE UNITED STATES OF AMERICA
13-205252-0 BC

How a Football-Control Strategy Can Help You Produce a Winning Team

Offensive football in recent years has shown a definite trend toward a wide-open attack with emphasis on the passing game. While this trend is desirable, the passing game should not be overemphasized to the neglect of the running game which we feel is fundamental to winning football. Only when a team has developed a proper run-pass balance in the attack will there be the needed flexibility for consistently winning football. Teams that neglect the running game normally do not play championship football.

One of the great advantages of a solid running game, properly balanced with a good passing game, is ball control. The ability of the offensive team to keep the football is a tremendous complement to a solid defensive team and is necessary for winning. For example, in one of Georgia's recent bowl games, our opponent was a team which led its offensive-minded conference in total yardage. In the bowl game, their total offensive production was 128 yards and no score. Their attack was built around a tremendous All-American running back who had a rushing average of over 100 yards a game. Against us he rushed for a total of 19 yards. While we played great defense in the game, the fact that we were able to keep the ball 45 of the 60 minutes was a big factor in the limited offensive production of our opponent. We had the ball a total of 85 plays to our opponent's 47. Their great running back carried the ball only seven times which was far below his average rushing attempts of 21 per game. By drastically reducing the play attempts of our opponent, the offense was a great complement to the defense, and was a big factor in our win.

While this book deals with offensive football, it is worthy to mention that in order for the offensive team to keep the football, it is necessary to have maximum opportunities of getting the football. This is where the defense must be offensive-minded. Defense must be a solid forcing effort that gets the football for the offense. The ability of our defense to force the opposition to give up the football by a kick, a fumble, or an interception has given the ball control game an opportunity to start functioning.

In addition to basic athletic talent, the true key to offensive football success lies in the ability of the coaching staff to teach individual players to execute the basic fundamentals. Therefore, the real test of coaching is teaching. It is not how much a coach knows about the game of football, but rather how effective he is in imparting this knowledge to his players and then motivating them to perform at their maximum. Proper organization of limited time, constructive corrective measures, and emphasis on the most important techniques are all vital to effective teaching. Constant repetition of the fundamental aspects of offensive football through appropriate drills is a must for proper execution.

All of the technical knowledge in football is worthless, however, unless it is applied with enthusiasm. Therefore, it is absolutely imperative that the basis for a winning emotion be established so that the morale of a football team is at its highest to properly carry out the technical aspects of the game. A winning emotion must be grounded on a broad and solid foundation. If a broad winning emotion is established, then the proper motivation is provided, and the offensive game has the intangible quality necessary to function effectively.

VINCE DOOLEY

Contents

At Georgia, we are convinced that we can and must win with a ball control type of offense featuring a tough ground game properly balanced by a strong passing game. In deciding on the type of offense to employ, the determining factor is personnel and not offensive philosophy. All of us must evaluate the players we have and be certain to base the offensive plan on what the individual players are capable of doing.

We believe that our squad must be strong physically. This means that our individual players must be in top physical condition and that we must be aggressive. And, above all, we must play an extremely consistent and error free type of game.

The "winning edge" in football can be found in many areas but we believe winning on offense can best be accomplished by having:

(1) *100% effort*—This simply means that each individual player gives everything

1

Rushing—The Heart
of the System

he has on every play, but more important, he gives that something extra in his second and even third efforts.

(2) *Consistency*—Enough cannot be said in this respect if a team
expects to win with a ground game based on ball control.
Stated as simply as possible, it means no penalties, broken
assignments, fumbles, or interceptions.

(3) *The ability to capitalize on opportunities*—On offense we must
take advantage of every changeover. This ability is especially
important on sudden changes resulting from pass interceptions,
recovered fumbles, or major penalties. You must score when
you get the ball close to the opponent's goal.

(4) *Desire to win*—Winning the game is everything, so we *must*
have something extra when we are behind or when we reach
the fourth quarter. It falls into three areas: conditioning, will
to win, and having special plays. When an offensive unit has
all three, it is physically conditioned, mentally conditioned, and
coached to get the job done within the rules of the game and
the physical capabilities of the players.

(5) *Strategy*—As simply stated as possible, the offense must know
how to play zone and field position football. This is primarily
a coaching responsibility; but it is the ultimate teaching job,
for the team must execute strategy for victory.

A ball-control offense must never give up the ball without scoring or
punting. It must be able to achieve extra performance in the danger
zones or when backed up near its own goal line. When the four down
zone is reached, it must score. And the entire squad must be disciplined
and dedicated to give great effort in downfield blocking—one downfield
block can produce a score.

To be successful in a ball-control game the number one obstacle to
overcome is inconsistency. Therefore, every play, every drill, and the
entire practice time are designed to assure perfection in execution. The
elimination of errors—fumbles, penalties, missed assignments, pass interceptions—is of prime consideration. These errors must not only be minimized but eliminated.

To maintain the ball control necessary for this type of game, each play
must average 4 yards per try. Again, consistency is the key to success
and for this reason, the passing game is held to a minimum. The third
and long situation must be avoided if opponents are to consider the run
first and foremost, and the pass second. The passing attack is of the

sprint-out and play-action type and is thrown on the so-called non-passing downs.

The ground game is not complicated or "fancy." Safe ball handling to insure proper execution with a minimum of errors is stressed. To accomplish the idea of ball control through consistency of execution, it is necessary to limit the attack to basic formations with limited plays. By this method, we strive for perfection.

When the basic attack has been mastered, the formations can be varied but the basic plays with regular blocking rules can be kept intact. In this way, the offensive "look" to some extent will be varied.

In addition to varying the formation, in any particular game a new variation of the attack may be used to afford a surprise element. These "specials" have over a period of years been very successful. Much time is spent in developing game-to-game "specials" for a particular opponent, but this is justified since the basic attack is somewhat limited.

Also, as a basic part of the running game, we use play action passes which are designed mainly as misdirection plays with the quarterback having the option to run or throw. Note that the first choice is to run. This type of play affords the opportunity for the "big" play and lends the much needed change-up in order to complicate defensive recognition. By using this type of play on the nonpassing downs, it is believed that to some extent the third down and long yardage situation can be avoided. The basic attack should be successful on third down and short yardage. After all, the third down situation is the key to successful ball control.

To summarize, the plan is as follows: (1) ball control through consistency and execution, (2) the use of basic formations, (3) a limited attack, (4) multiple formations and special plays for variation, and (5) play action passes with first option to run.

The Georgia Running Game

To accomplish the above objective of ball control, the number one formation has been the tight slot formation. Most teams today tend to go to a more "pro-type" look utilizing one or more players in a flanking position, but we have developed a balanced attack with strength both to and away from the slot.

The tight slot affords a balanced offense. Rather than flanking a back, the slotback is used as a power blocker first and then as a runner and a pass receiver. For example, the slotback double teams for the power play off tackle, leads blocks on the linebacker on isolation plays, cut-blocks for the quarterback sprint-outs, and blocks downfield on all other running plays where he is not the ballcarrier or a key faking back. Of course he is the pitch man on the outside belly and split "T" options.

The basic tight slot formation is diagrammed below:

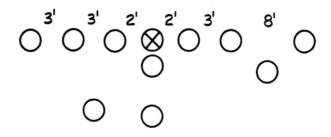

Figure 1–1. *The alignment of the tight slot forma-tion.*

Normal splits are 2 feet between guards and center and 3 feet between guards and tackles and between tackle and end. The slot is approximately 8 feet in width. These splits may vary in order to accomplish the job. This is called taking a "working distance" split. "Working distance" is the split necessary to get the job done. In general, the "working distance" is a maximum split for inside plays and a minimum split for outside plays. For example, the tackle would take a maximum split for the split "T" handoff while taking a minimum split for the outside belly option.

There are many blocking schemes, rules, numbering of the defenses, etc., and knowing whom to block certainly comes first in any offensive attack, but you must not only know whom to block but how to block him. The first step in blocking techniques is the proper split, and therefore, "working distance" is of major importance.

In order to execute any offensive play, players must first recognize the defense and know the various blocking assignments. Blocking is the key to offensive football and knowing which defender to block is the first step.

We number the various defenses and designate them as "odd" or "even." An "odd" defense will have a defender lined up on the offensive center. If no one is on the offensive center, the defense is an "even" one. Generally, in an "odd" defense, the linebackers have odd numbers. Similarly in "even" defenses, they have even numbers.

The numbering of the defense then starts by numbering a defender on the offensive center as "0." The first defender on either side of the center is designated by #1, the second #2, the third #3, and the fourth #4. We further designate the side to which the play is to be run as the "onside" and the side away from the point of attack as the "offside." This is particularly helpful in attacking "stack" defenses where the linebacker is directly behind a lineman.

The most widely used defenses are diagrammed and numbered in the following figures. (See Figures 1–2 through 1–11.)

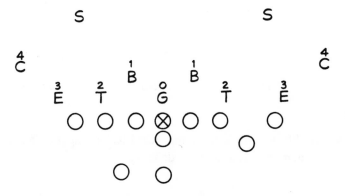

Figure 1–2. *The numbering of the basic 5–2 defense.*

Figure 1–3. *The numbering of the basic 5–4 eagle defense.*

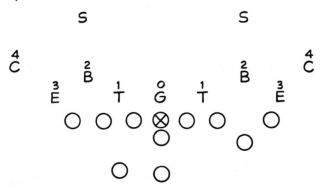

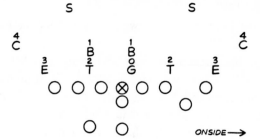

Figure 1–4. *The numbering of the stack defense (odd).*

NOTE: When a stack is in the guard-center gap on the onside, we number this as an odd defense.

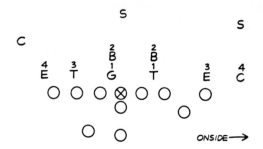

Figure 1–5. *The numbering of the stack defense (even).*

NOTE: When a stack is in the guard-tackle gap on the onside, we number this as an even defense.

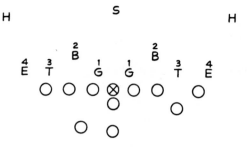

Figure 1–6. *The numbering of the loose tackle six defense.*

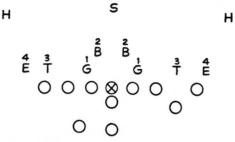

Figure 1-7. *The numbering of the split six defense.*

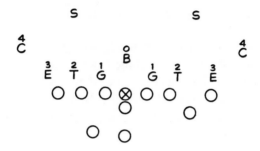

Figure 1-8. *The numbering of the 6-3 defense.*

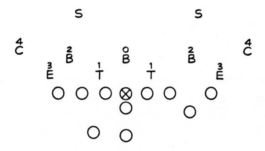

Figure 1-9. *The numbering of the 4-3 defense.*

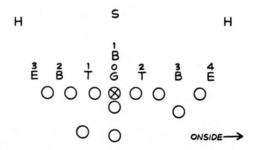

Figure 1-10. *The numbering of the 7-1 defense.*

7

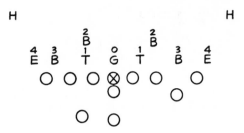

Figure 1–11. *The numbering of the 7–4 defense.*

Once the decision is made concerning what type of blocking rules the offense will use and, in the case of the Georgia offense, once the various opposition defenses have been numbered for rule purposes, the next step is to decide what plays will constitute the basic offense attack.

The Georgia offensive attack is grouped in series, and there are six basic ones numbered as follows:

> 10's Sprint out pass and quarterback keep.
> 20's Split T series.
> 30's Quick trap series.
> 40's Power sweep series.
> 50's Inside belly series.
> 60's Outside belly series.

The hole numbering system utilizes the even numbers to the right and odd numbers to the left as diagrammed below:

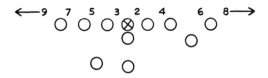

Figure 1–12. *The hole number system.*

The wide plays are the "8" and "9" holes while "6" and "7" holes are off-tackle, etc. We differ from other numbering systems in that our inside numbers "2" and "3" indicate trap blocking, unless otherwise designated by an added call such as wedge or counter which indicates another type of blocking.

We do not believe that an entire series must be used, but we strongly believe that a balanced attack must be presented from a basic formation.

The following plays will be diagrammed to attack both the "loose six" and the "52 monster" defenses, and the rules used to block the various defenses will be described.

It should be noted that the actual plays used in any series are determined by: (1) the special abilities of our present personnel, and (2) the particular strengths or weaknesses of the opponent.

Sprint Out Series: We run only one basic running play in this series, and it is the quarterback sweep or the sprint out keep. It attacks the corner quickly with maximum blocking and affords the threat of a pass. The line will use minimum splits ("working distance"), and the corner will in effect be attacked with a "double team" block. This is accomplished by the slotback using a reach block technique while the tailback uses quick motion in order to be in position to cut back on the end and to clean up the block by the slotback.

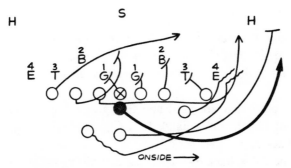

Figure 1–13. *The quarterback sprint out keep vs. the loose tackle six defense.*

Figure 1–14. *The quarterback sprint out keep vs. the 5–2 defense.*

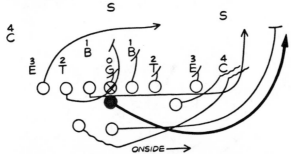

Blocking rules for quarterback sweep (sprint keep):

Onside End—Drive #3.

Onside Tackle—Drive #2.

Onside Guard—Drive #1.

Center—Drive #0; None there—drive #1 offside.

Offside Guard—Pull flat, turn up, and seal. (*Coaching Point:* pick up any penetration of the line of scrimmage.)

Offside Tackle—Check second man from center on or off the line of scrimmage and release.

Offside End—Release inside #3 for safety.

Quarterback—Open with lead step and attack the corner quickly. (*Coaching Point:* get in fullback's hip pocket.)

Fullback—Run an arc on the defensive halfback and block him anywhere he goes.

Slotback—Reach block first man outside offensive end. (*Coaching Point:* attack his outside knee.)

Tailback—Quick motion and cut-block first man outside onside end. (*Coaching Point:* double team with slotback.)

This play will be further discussed in Chapter 6. (See Chapter 6, Figures 6–5 and 6–6.)

The Split T Series: The split T series will allow a team to make good use of a quick, fast-charging offensive line and a good running quarterback. This series can be used effectively against both odd and even defenses.

Three plays that are used and that give effective balance from this series are: (1) the quick handoff, (2) the fullback counter, and (3) the quarterback option play.

1. The quick handoff—This is a fast-hitting, straight-ahead type of play that allows a back to run to "daylight" behind one-on-one blocking. The success of the play depends upon: (1) good line spacing, (2) an explosive line charge, and (3) a back who has the knack for seeing and running to an opening.

Figure 1–15. *The quick handoff vs. the loose tackle six defense.*

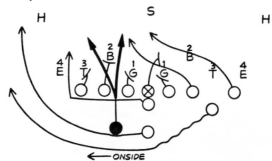

←—ONSIDE

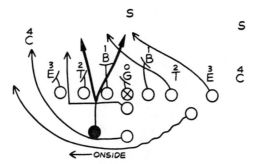

Figure 1–16. *The quick handoff vs. the 5–2 defense.*

Blocking rules for the quick handoff:

> *Onside End*—Drive #3, if he is outside, release and block halfback.
> *Onside Tackle*—Drive #2.
> *Onside Guard*—Drive #1.
> *Center*—Odd drive #0, even drive offside linebacker.
> *Offside Guard*—Drive #1.
> *Offside Tackle*—Release inside #2, block at point of attack.
> *Offside End*—Release, block at point of attack.
> *Quarterback*—Jab step up into line and hand off to tailback. Fake the quarterback option.
> *Fullback*—Fake the quarterback option.
> *Slotback*—"Fly" and fake the quarterback option.
> *Tailback*—Take the handoff, "read" the defense, and run to "daylight."

2. The fullback counter—This play is an inside play designed for use after the quick handoff has been established as an offensive threat and the defense is pursuing to stop the quick handoff.

On this play, the quarterback takes the ball and fakes a handoff to the halfback, turns, and gives the ball to the fullback who has taken a counter-step and is breaking up the middle. The counter-step creates misdirection and tends to keep the defense at home, thus minimizing quick pursuit.

Figure 1–17. *The fullback counter vs. the loose tackle six defense.*

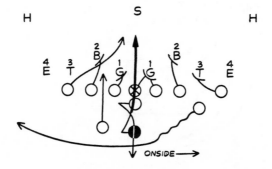

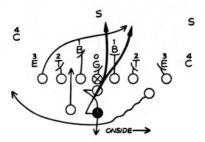

Figure 1–18. *The fullback counter vs. the 5–2 defense.*

Rules for the fullback counter:

> *Onside End*—Drive #3, if #3 is outside release, block at point of attack.
> *Onside Tackle*—Drive #2.
> *Onside Guard*—Drive #1.
> *Center*—Drive #0, even lead on #1 on the onside.
> *Offside Guard*—Drive #1.
> *Offside Tackle*—Drive #2.
> *Offside End*—Release inside #3, block at point of attack.
> *Quarterback*—Jab step into line and half-step toward diving tailback; pivot back into line and handoff to fullback. After handoff, drop back and fake pass.
> *Fullback*—Counter-step to left, then drive for right hip of center. **Cut off** of the center's block.
> *Slotback*—Run quarterback option fake.
> *Tailback*—Fake handoff to outside hip of guard, drop inside shoulder.

3. The quarterback option play—This option play is an off tackle or wide play for use after the quick handoff has been established. On this play, the quarterback fakes the quick handoff play (to hold the inside defense); he then continues down the line of scrimmage and options the defensive corner; that is, he keeps the ball and runs off tackle, *or* he pitches the ball to the slotback who is circling wide.

Figure 1–19. *The quarterback option play vs. the loose tackle six defense.*

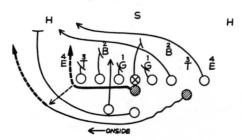

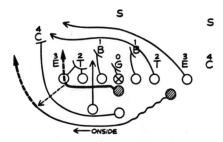

Figure 1–20. *The quarterback option play vs. the 5–2 defense.*

Rules for the quarterback option play:

Onside End—Even drive #3, odd lead on #2.
Onside Tackle—Even drive #2, odd post #2.
Onside Guard—Drive #1.
Center—Odd drive #0, even block offside linebacker.
Offside Guard—Drive #1.
Offside Tackle—Release inside #2, block at point of attack.
Offside End—Release, block at point of attack.
Quarterback—Jab step into line and fake handoff. Read the defensive end and keep off tackle or pitch to slotback wide.
Fullback—Run an arc for outside leg of widest defender. Block him any way he goes.
Tailback—Fake the handoff and seal the gap outside of the tackle.
Slotback—Fly and run outside looking for the pitch. Use the fullback's block.

These three basic plays afford a balanced attack from our basic slot formation and utilize the particular running abilities of each of the backs.

The Quick Trap Series: The quick trap series allows a team to run inside with trap blocking. This is effective when the defense is penetrating the line of scrimmage with defensive linemen in order to stop or pressure the offense.

The quick series requires quick guards and an aggressive, tough running fullback.

There are two basic plays off this series: (1) the fullback trap, and (2) the halfback counter trap.

Figure 1–21. *The fullback trap vs. the loose tackle six defense.*

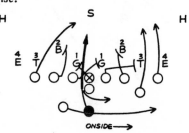

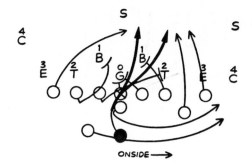

Figure 1–22. *The fullback trap vs. the 5–2 defense.*

(1) The fullback trap—Rules for the fullback trap are:

> *Onside End*—Release, block at point of attack.
> *Onside Tackle*—Odd: drive near linebacker, even: block near LB.
> *Onside Guard*—Odd: drive #0, even: influence #1 and block first man outside on line of scrimmage.
> *Center*—Odd: post #0, even: drive #1 offside.
> *Offside Guard*—Pull and drive first man on line of scrimmage beyond the center.
> *Offside Tackle*—Cut off first man outside offguard.
> *Offside End*—Release, block at the point of attack.
> *Slotback*—Release over right tackle block downfield.
> *Tailback*—Fake sweep wide to the onside.
> *Fullback*—Carry, run off right hip of center.
> *Quarterback*—Reverse out, hand off to fullback, fake wide to onside.

(2) The halfback counter trap—This play serves as a counter after the fullback trap has been established and the defense is pinching in when the fullback starts up the middle.

The play is designed to trap the first defensive man in the slot.

Figure 1–23. *The halfback counter trap vs. the loose tackle six defense.*

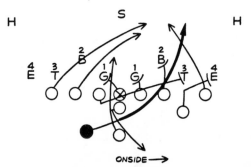

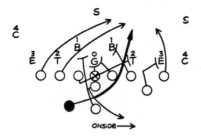

Figure 1–24. *The halfback counter trap vs. the 5–2 defense.*

Rules for the halfback counter trap:

Onside End—Even: release block halfback, odd: drive #1.

Onside Tackle—Drive near linebacker. (*Coaching Point:* vs. eagle double team with guard on #1.)

Center—Odd: drive #0, even: drive #1 offside.

Offside Guard—Pull drive first man outside onside tackle.

Offside Tackle—Release inside #2 block at the point of attack.

Offside End—Release block at the point of attack.

Slotback—Influence inside man in slot turnout on first man on the line of scrimmage.

Left Halfback—Carry and take pulling guards block.

Fullback—Fake over the left hip of the center. Fill the area.

Quarterback—Fake to fullback, give to halfback, then fake pass.

The Power Sweep Series: The power sweep series requires excellent double team blocking and a good blocking fullback. The plays afford concentrated power at the point of attack.

There are two basic plays: (1) the off tackle power, and (2) the wide power sweep.

(1) The off tackle power—This is a good play against any defense and serves well as a short yardage play. It is the "bread and butter" play of the offense, and the point of attack is the slot.

Figure 1–25. *The off tackle power vs. the loose tackle six defense.*

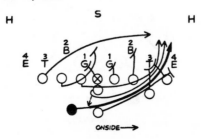

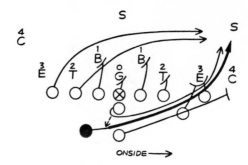

Figure 1–26. *The off tackle power vs. the 5–2 defense.*

Rules for the off tackle power sweep:

>*Onside End*—Drive #3 unless outside, if #3 is outside block #2.
>*Onside Tackle*—Drive #2, if #3 is outside end post #2.
>*Onside Guard*—Drive #1.
>*Center*—Odd: drive #0, even: drive #1 offside.
>*Offside Guard*—Even: pull lead ballcarrier through hole. (*Coaching Point:* look for penetration.) Odd: drive #1.
>*Offside Tackle*—Even: pull behind guard, turn up over the center, fill for guard. Odd: release inside #2 block at point of attack.
>*Offside End*—Release, block safety.
>*Slotback*—Double team on #3; if #3 is outside end, lead on #2.
>*Left Halfback*—Carry and hug double team block.
>*Fullback*—Lead step for first man outside offensive end.
>*Quarterback*—Reverse pivot and pitch to tailback, lead through hole, and block defensive halfback.

(2) The wide power sweep—This play is used after the off tackle power has been established. The idea is to hook the defensive end or corner defender after forcing him to close hard to help stop the power off tackle play. It is essential from a personnel point of view that the running back have good speed.

Figure 1–27. *The wide power sweep vs. the loose tackle six defense.*

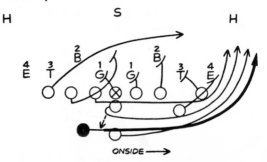

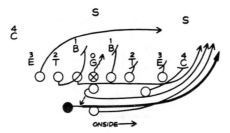

Figure 1–28. *The wide power sweep vs. the 5–2 defense.*

Rules for the wide power sweep:

Onside End—Drive #3.
Onside Tackle—Drive #2.
Onside Guard—Drive #1.
Center—Odd: drive #0, even: drive #1 offside.
Offside Guard—Pull, lead ballcarrier wide. (*Coaching Point:* look for penetration.)
Offside Tackle—Pull behind guard, turn upfield over center, fill for guard.
Offside End—Release, block at the point of attack.
Slotback—Block first man outside offensive end.
Tailback—Carry, read fullback's block on #4.
Fullback—Run arc on outside leg of widest defender and block him anywhere he goes.
Quarterback—Reverse out, pitch to left halfback, lead ballcarrier wide.

The Inside Belly Series: This series is designed to isolate an interior defender (usually a linebacker), and then run the fullback with a halfback leading him into the hole. A good blocking halfback and a tough running fullback are necessary for success with this type of play series.

There are three inside plays off this series: (1) the isolation play to the fullback, (2) the halfback trap, and (3) the counter trap.

Figure 1–29. *The isolation play to the fullback vs. the loose tackle six defense.*

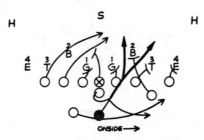

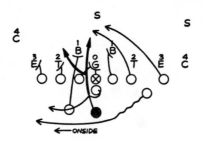

Figure 1–30. *The isolation play to the fullback vs. the 5–2 defense.*

(1) The isolation play to the fullback—This play is one of the fastest hitting power plays in our attack and is one of the basic short yardage and goal line plays. Rules for the isolation play:

> *Onside End*—Block first man outside. (*Coaching Point:* if two men in slot, cut off widest man.)
>
> *Onside Tackle*—Block first man outside; if outside end, block man nearest you.
>
> *Onside Guard*—Odd: drive #0, even: drive #1.
>
> *Center*—Odd: drive #0, even: block offside linebacker.
>
> *Offside Guard*—Drive #1.
>
> *Offside Tackle*—Release inside #2, block at point of attack.
>
> *Offside End*—Release, block at the point of attack.
>
> *Slotback*—Block near linebacker if onside; offside—"fly."
>
> *Tailback*—Fake wide sweep to onside unless leading on linebacker.
>
> *Fullback*—Carry at inside hip of onside tackle, read slotback block.
>
> *Quarterback*—Reverse out, hand off to fullback, continue on around end.

(2) The halfback trap—After the defense braces to stop the isolation play to the fullback, a good counterplay is to fake the handoff to the fullback, pivot, and hand off to the halfback breaking up the middle behind trap blocking.

Figure 1–31. *The halfback trap vs. the loose tackle six defense.*

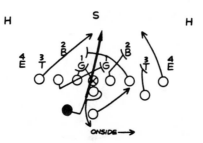

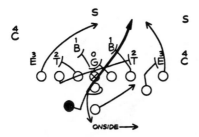

Figure 1–32. *The halfback trap vs. the 5–2 defense.*

Rules for the halfback trap:

> *Onside End*—Release, block at the point of attack.
>
> *Onside Tackle*—Even: block across ball to first linebacker, odd: drive near linebacker.
>
> *Onside Guard*—Even: influence and drive first man outside, odd: lead on #0.
>
> *Center*—Even: lead on #1 offside, odd; post #0, check off linebacker.
>
> *Offside Guard*—Drive #1 on line of scrimmage.
>
> *Offside Tackle*—Pull and trap first man on the line of scrimmage beyond center.
>
> *Offside End*—Cut off #3 unless outside then release, block at the point of attack.
>
> *Quarterback*—Fake to fullback, pivot, hand off to halfback breaking up middle, fake wide.
>
> *Tailback*—Lead step with right foot, drive up middle, inside quarterback running close to trap block.
>
> *Slotback*—Fake lead block, cut off tackle, block downfield.
>
> *Fullback*—Fake isolation play and block first man on line of scrimmage.

Figure 1–33. *The counter trap vs. the loose tackle six defense.*

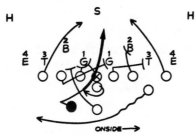

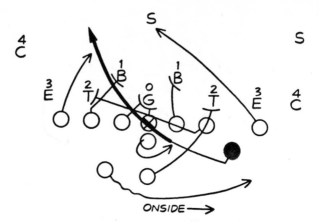

Figure 1-34. *The counter trap vs. 5–2 defense.*

(3) The counter trap—Rules for the counter trap are:

Onside End—Release, block halfback onside.

Onside Tackle—Drive near linebacker.

Onside Guard—Even: influence and turn out on first man on the line of scrimmage, odd: drive #0.

Center—Even: lead on #1 offside, odd: drive #0.

Offside Guard—Drive #1.

Offside Tackle—Pull drive first on line of scrimmage beyond center.

Offside End—Release, block at point of attack.

Slotback—Even: fake wide play offside; odd: drive second man in slot.

Fullback—Fill for pulling tackle.

Tailback—Counter-step, break up middle inside quarterback carry, hug tackles, trap block.

Quarterback—Reverse pivot, fake to fullback, hand off to tailback, continue on around end offside.

The Outside Belly Series: The outside belly series completes offensive balance in that it provides a means of getting off tackle with the fullback behind power blocking and gives the quarterback a wide option play after faking the fullback off tackle.

A team needs the complement of a good running fullback and quarterback to make this series successful. The two plays that are commonly used in the outside belly series are these: (1) the fullback off tackle, (2) the outside belly option play.

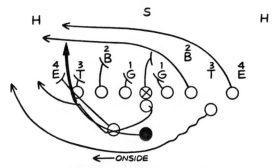

Figure 1–35. *The fullback off tackle vs. the loose tackle six defense.*

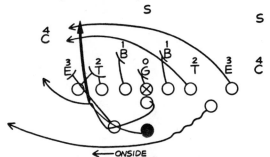

Figure 1–36. *The fullback off tackle vs. the 5–2 defense.*

(1) The fullback off tackle—Rules for the fullback off tackle play:

Onside End—Drive #3 unless outside, then lead on #2.
Onside Tackle—Even: drive #2, odd: post #1 on line of scrimmage.
Onside Guard—Odd: drive #1, even: drive #1.
Center—Odd: drive #0, even: block offside linebacker.
Offside Guard—Drive #1.
Offside Tackle—Release inside #2 block at the point of attack.
Offside End—Release, block at the point of attack.
Quarterback—Reverse pivot and hand off to fullback, fake option play.
Slotback—Fake option play.
Tailback—Drive first man outside offensive end.
Fullback—Carry over outside hip of offensive end.

(2) The outside belly option play—After the fullback off tackle play has been established and the defensive corner is bracing to stop this play, the outside belly option play provides a good change of pace.

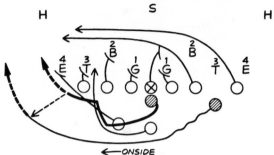

Figure 1–37. *The outside belly option play vs. the loose tackle six defense.*

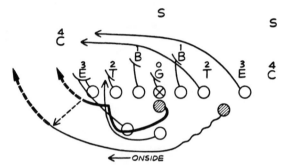

Figure 1–38. *The outside belly option play vs. the 5–2 defense.*

Rules for the outside belly option play:

> *Onside End*—Drive #3.
> *Onside Tackle*—Even: drive #2, odd: drive #1 on line of scrimmage.
> *Onside Guard*—Drive #1.
> *Center*—Odd: drive #0, even: drive off linebacker.
> *Offside Guard*—Cut off #1.
> *Offside Tackle*—Release inside #2 block at the point of attack.
> *Offside End*—Release, block at the point of attack.
> *Quarterback*—Make quick fake to FB, option the defensive corner.
> *Slotback*—Lead step, give ground slightly, and look for the pitch.
> *Tailback*—Block widest man on line of scrimmage.
> *Fullback*—Fake fullback off tackle play.

On the previous pages are included the plays that constitute the basic Georgia running game. These plays make up about 95 per cent of the running attack. Certain backfield patterns can be mixed with different basic blocking schemes in order to get the strongest possible play. For example, the halfback counter trap backfield action off the quick trap series may be combined with isolation type blocking to strengthen the play against certain teams. (See Figure 1–39.)

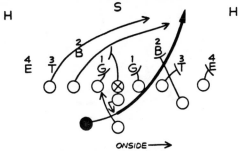

Figure 1–39. *The halfback counter trap combined with isolation blocking vs. loose tackle six defense.*

Special Plays

In each game plan are included a few "special" running plays. These plays are designed to give the offense a change of pace and a much needed gain in clutch situations. Statistics have shown that the best special plays have been off tackle or wide plays in situations where the defense might hesitate in adjusting to a new formation, or in situations where the defense may make the wrong adjustments. The offense must be careful in selecting such formations so that the desired effect will be realized.

It is important that basic backfield patterns and blocking schemes be used so that a minimum of practice time is required to get the play ready. The most important factor in the use of such plays is that the offensive team must be taught to *hustle out of the huddle, line up quickly,* and run the play on a quick count before the defense has a chance to react and adjust.

In the following illustrations are diagrammed "specials" that have been used with success: (1) the wide power sweep, and (2) the quarterback sprint keep.

(1) The wide power sweep—The formation from which this play is run is an unbalanced tight slot set with the fullback "cheated" over toward the slot. The offside end is brought over and split out on the slot

side. The tailback is put in quick motion and the quarterback flips the
ball to him.

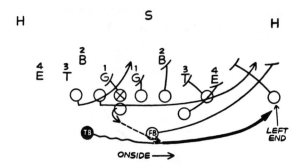

Figure 1–40. *The special wide power sweep vs.
loose tackle six defense.*

(2) The quarterback sprint keep—Several formations can be used
from which to run a special quarterback keep, but one that has been
used with success is a wide slot with the tailback lined up about halfway
from the slotback to the split end.

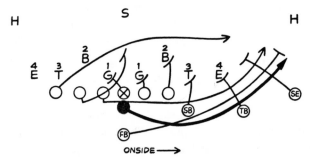

Figure 1–41. *The special quarterback sprint keep
vs. the loose tackle six defense.*

Diversified Sets

In order to give the offense a new look, different sets are employed
but the same basic plays and essentially the same blocking schemes
are used. (See Figure 1–42.)

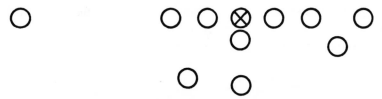

Figure 1–42. *The tight slot with split end.*

In this set, nothing is changed to the strong side. On the weak side, a split end is used which tends to strengthen the passing game, and therefore force defensive adjustments.

From the slot set, the backs might "slide" or go to a "strong" set. (See Figures 1–43 and 1–44.)

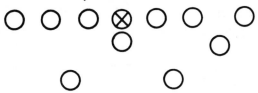

Figure 1–43. *The tight slot with a "slide" back-field.*

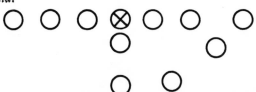

Figure 1–44. *The tight slot with a "strong" back-field.*

To the strong side a "wide slot" can be used. This particular set provides the possibility of a good sprint-out attack as well as the outside belly option play to the formation side. (See Figure 1–45.)

Figure 1–45. *The wide slot.*

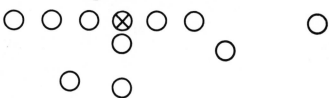

Again the front can be varied with a split end and the backs lined up in the "I" formation. In this set, the basic inside game and blocking schemes remain the same. (See Figure 1–46.)

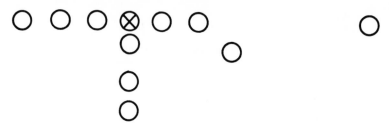

Figure 1–46. *The "I" formation with a wide slot.*

Over a period of several games, a large number of sets may be shown. Therefore, opponents must work on a number of defensive adjustments while the offense is still working on a basic ground attack, just eliminating those plays which cannot be run because of the split end or the different alignment of the backs.

Offensive beliefs and philosophy are only so many X's and O's until plans are formulated for teaching techniques and developing the necessary execution needed for success.

A great deal of time must be put in daily in order to have an adequate and workable practice plan. The major part of the working day goes into planning the practice schedule.

The general breakdown concerning the time and the periods is the prerogative of the head coach, but the practice utilization of these time periods is left up to the individual offensive and defensive coaches. The major part of each morning is used to determine the best utilization of the limited time available for practice. Fighting the battle of "too little time" is one of the biggest concerns facing a coaching staff.

Assistant coaches must be sound teachers. It certainly is not how much the coaches know about the game, but rather how well they can teach

2

Practice—Organization Leads to Winning Ball-Control Execution

individual players to execute the offense. In order to facilitate this teaching job, a well-planned practice schedule is essential.

Every phase of offensive football must be covered. To be sure of this, each position coach on the staff has a checklist which is checked daily so that he can be sure that he is teaching what is believed necessary for winning. It might be a very simple form that would look something like this for the offensive line coach. (See Figure 2–1.)

Figure 2–1. *Fundamentals and techniques checklist for the offensive linemen.*

Dates	9-1	9-2	9-3	9-4			
Set! Set! Set!	✓	✓	✓	✓			
Hit! Hit! Hit!	✓	✓	✓	✓			
Board drill	✓	✓	✓	✓			
One-on-one block	✓	✓	✓				
Cutoff block	✓	✓					
Reach block	✓	✓					
Bootleg block	✓	✓					
Oklahoma drill		✓	✓				
Inside drill			✓				
Half-line scrimmage			✓				
Scrimmage				✓			
Punt protection	✓	✓	✓	✓			

All positional coaches have checklists like the above abbreviated sample, and the list should include all basic fundamental drills and techniques used by each coach in football practice.

The head coach should have an overall checklist that covers all phases of the game.

Each coach should keep a scrimmage and game grade chart for his men in order to trace development of individual players.

The Prepractice Meeting

As mentioned above, for a coach to be successful, he must be a successful teacher. Every day the squad has a prepractice meeting in order for the coach to "teach" that day's work. First, the players know what is to be expected of them on a given day. Second, they are taught assignments, stances, blocks, techniques, and anything else concerning the offense. This saves time on the practice field, as time on the practice field should be used in execution and repetition rather than in conversation. The best teaching is accomplished by exposing the players to as much football as possible—lectures, blackboard talks, films, demonstrations, actual drills, and individual execution of techniques. We provide the best in equipment in order to motivate each boy to perform at the peak of his ability.

The squad should meet briefly with the head coach and then break up into small positional groups—line, ends, and backs, for individual meetings with the position coach. This occurs *every day* during spring practice and *every day* during the regular season.

These meetings are rarely longer than 25 minutes and can be beneficial if as short as ten minutes. It is important for players not only to execute their assignments, but also to understand the offense and to know why it must be executed in a certain way. Teaching football is salesmanship in the truest sense. Players must be sold upon the idea that your way is not only the best way, but the only way to win.

The squad should be dressed for practice with the exception of their shoes for these prepractice meetings. Five minutes is allowed for getting to the practice field. This time is actually shown on the practice schedule, and everyone is expected to remain on this schedule. (See Figure 2–2 for practice schedule.)

In the sample practice schedule below, each position coach will spell out in detail the exact techniques, plays, etc. that will be worked on during each time period.

These schedules are filed, and by referring to them along with the daily checklists, a smooth, organized, complete coaching job is easier to achieve.

Figure 2–2. *The offensive practice schedule.*

		LINE	ENDS	BACKS
Meet	3:30—3:45	ASSIGNMENTS ———————————→		
Shoes	3:45—4:00	———————————→		
Specialty	4:00—4:15	ASSIGNMENTS & TECHNIQUES	ALL PASS & SPRINT OUT ———→	
Calisthenics, 2–S	4:15—4:25	CAL, 2-S	DRILL ————————→	
Fundamentals	4:25—4:40	SET, SET, SET BOARDS, ONE	ON ONE→	OBSTACLE COURSE
Group	4:40—4:50	½ LINE SCRIMMAGE ————→		
Kicking	4:50—5:00	PUNT PROTECTION + COVERAGE →		
Pass	5:00—5:15	PLAY ACTION PASSES ————→		
Team	5:15—5:35	RUNNING OFFENSE ————→		
Sprints	5:35—5:40	———————————→		

Practice Fields and Equipment

The football practice field is divided into offensive and defensive fields. (See Figure 2–3.)

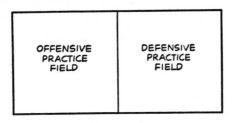

Figure 2–3. *Practice area divided into offensive and defensive fields.*

The offensive field is divided into three areas: (1) offensive ends, (2) offensive backs, and (3) offensive line. Each group, its practice equipment, and its arrangement is shown in Figure 2–4.

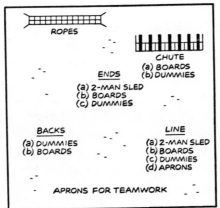

Figure 2–4. *Arrangement of equipment on the offensive field.*

Offensive practice equipment and pieces needed:

    (1) Two 2-man sleds.
    (2) Fifteen boards (12 feet x 10 inches x 2 inches—beveled edges).
    (3) One 7-man blocking chute (see 2-S drill page 36).
    (4) Ropes.
    (5) Eleven aprons.
    (6) Fifteen dummies.

The practice field should have all the equipment necessary to teach individual techniques. Fortunately most of the equipment is not expensive when you think of it in terms of the number of years it is used rather than its initial cost.

A designated assistant coach has the responsibility of coordinating practice equipment needs every day with a student manager. The student manager checks with this coach each day prior to practice and then makes sure that the proper equipment is ready and placed when the football team takes the field for practice.

Specialty Period

The specialty period follows the prepractice meeting. This is used as a teaching period with the emphasis being placed on technique, and it should be a more relaxed time than any other in the practice schedule. This is especially true in the latter part of the season when the weather is cold and there is danger of pulling muscles without sufficient warm-up. The entire squad should come on the field running. The quarterbacks have footballs to pass back and forth to each other as they run, the backs carry footballs, and all players run through the ropes to loosen up their legs as they go to the offensive field.

The backs and ends start their specialty period with an "all pass" drill. How the quarterback carries the ball up, his delivery, his follow-through, and his call of "ball" to indicate coverage to the entire team is stressed in the drill. The "Baylor" idea of throwing with the point up, an exaggerated quickness in carrying the ball up, and the follow-through turning the palm down after throwing are coaching points to stress. The receivers should work on concentration and "pride" in catching the football. The receivers should concentrate on using their hands; they should stress seeing the ball and keeping the hands out of the way of the eyes until the last possible second. In other words, receivers should not run with arms and hands up. Finally, the receivers should use an exaggerated look at the ball as the ball is put away under the arm.

Each quarterback is placed with a group of four or five receivers, and by using two footballs per group, each group is able to throw and catch a large number of passes in a short time. The quarterbacks then change to the other side of their line and now throw to the same receivers from the opposite side. The drill is completed by throwing an over-the-shoulder, going-away type pass. For example—a deep route. Again, the receiver works to keep his hands in a normal running position until the last possible second. This drill is diagrammed and described in the chapter on end play. (See Chapter 5, page 130.)

When this five-minute period is complete, the fullbacks report to the backfield coach for work on pass protection blocking—sprint out and pull up types. During this time, emphasis is placed on assignments and techniques under controlled conditions. The blocking drills are against men with dummies or men in aprons, in order to protect the players from injuries.

During the second five minutes, the ends, slotbacks, and tailbacks work on special pass routes, starting with what is termed the "hot" receiver drill which is designed to beat blitzing or firing linebackers. (See Figure 2–5.)

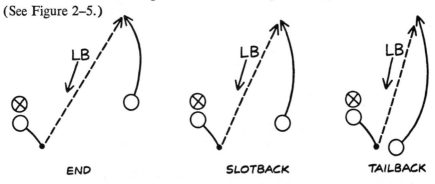

 END   SLOTBACK   TAILBACK

Figure 2–5. *The hot receiver drill.*

The hot receiver drill is a skeleton drill with the linebacker actually blitzing and the quarterback delivering the ball immediately to the "hot" receiver. This is a method of combating the blitz and is a way to put the receiver immediately into an open-field running situation.

The next five minutes are used by tailbacks and fullbacks for play polish while the ends and slotbacks run regular routes. These routes will be discussed in the chapter on end play. (See Chapter 5, pages 132–137.)

These regular routes are run against a dummy defense using a certain coverage. To pass successfully, it is obvious that an accurate passer and and a good receiver are essential; but protection is our first concern, and our second concern is the coverage. It is impossible to have a passing game if the passer and receivers cannot recognize and beat the defensive coverage; thus, we spend time daily to work on recognition of defensive secondary coverage.

During the specialty period, the interior offensive linemen work on defensive recognition and blocking techniques. Remember, this is a specialty period and is not full speed, but a relaxed, teaching situation. The defenses we expect to face when we play our next opponent are reviewed, with special emphasis on any unusual alignment of defenders or any special stunts. Regular rules and blocking calls are reviewed along with recognition of stunts. For example, the line coach can line up in the quarterback position and call out the desired offensive play. From this position he can signal to the defense the stunt and alignment that he wants. He then calls out the starting count, takes the snap from the center, and checks assignments and techniques. (See Figure 2–6.)

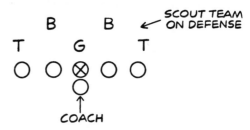

Figure 2–6. *The offensive line coach checking assignments and techniques during specialty period.*

Linemen and backs are taught during the specialty period to transfer material learned in the prepractice classroom teaching session into actual execution. The "know whom" and "know how" theories of the proper techniques of blocking, ball handling, passing, receiving, and the recognition of defensive alignments and coverages are put into practice.

Exercise Period

The squad exercises five minutes together with the week's game captains as exercise leaders. Exercises will not be described, but leg stretching and neck bridging exercises are the ones stressed. Because we have experienced trouble with pulled muscles, everything possible is done to avoid this type of injury. Neck bridging increases the strength of the neck muscles. This period ends with a quick and spirited grass drill to get the remainder of the practice started in the proper tempo. The remaining five minutes of the exercise period is used by our defense to work on agility while the offensive teams work on the 2–S drill.

2-S Drill (Stance and Starts)

We use this full team drill early in each practice session with the main objectives being these: (1) proper huddle (See Figure 2–7), (2) proper huddle discipline (being attentive, etc.), (3) proper breaking of the huddle, (4) hustling to the ball to line up, (5) correct offensive stance, and (6) exploding on the snap. This drill also doubles as a tempo-setter for practice because it requires much concentration, discipline, and hustle and we hope this attitude will carry over into other drills for the day.

In this drill (See Figure 2–8), we use a device made of iron pipe that serves to keep the offensive linemen from raising up too soon. (See Figure 2–9.) This device has seven stalls—one for each offensive lineman. In each stall we place a board (12 feet long, 10 inches wide, 2 inches thick, and beveled on one side) and on each of these boards is placed a stand-up dummy held by a man. At the ends of this device we can line up men holding dummies lined up as true ends, defensive halfbacks, etc. A ball is placed in front of the middle stall.

With the men and equipment in position, using teams, we work on option and sweep type plays, with the seven offensive linemen concentrating on lining up *on the ball,* assuming a good stance, exploding on the snap, and blocking the dummies down and off the end of the boards. The backs work on correct alignment, getting an explosive start, correct execution of the play called, and blocking on the defensive corners.

One team will huddle up 6 yards from the ball, call a play, break the huddle, hustle to the ball, line up on the ball, and run the play. As soon as one team has run a play and all men have completed their assignments, a second team can be huddling to repeat the procedure.

Coaching tips: The backfield coach checks on the huddle, huddle discipline, the calling of the play, the proper breaking of the huddle, the stance and alignment of the backs, and backfield execution and blocking. The line coach checks to see that each lineman glances in at the ball as he lines up, assumes a close-to-the-ball alignment, gets set quickly, assumes a correct stance, and that all seven explode out *together* using proper blocking techniques on the dummies. He also makes sure that all men hustle back to run another play.

In about five minutes, 20 plays can be run if the tempo is fast enough.

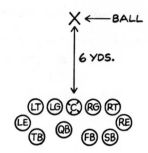

Figure 2–7. *Huddle.*

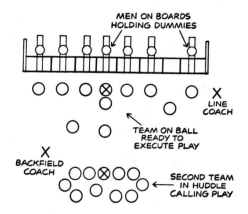

Figure 2–8. *Top view of 2–S drill.*

Figure 2–9. *Views and dimensions of seven-man blocking chute.*

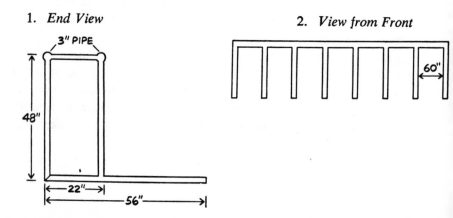

1. *End View*   2. *View from Front*

Fundamental and Group Work

During fundamental and group work, the offensive coaches will separate into groups with their respective personnel. The end coach will take the ends; the interior line coach will take the tackles, guards, and centers; and the backfield coach will take the backs.

This particular time is basically devoted to fundamentals. Flexibility in planning is necessary for emphasis on certain needs, such as our passing game or play polish for our backs. However, the nucleus of this period is used primarily for developing and improving blocking and movement. All types of drills are used to accomplish this objective. (Drills are discussed in more detail in Chapters 3, 4, and 5.)

During the football season, the fundamentals of blocking, ball handling, and running techniques are stressed during group work. We can also use this period to install any new running plays or blocking techniques not fully covered in the specialty period. However, fundamentals are the primary purpose of this period. Each group has a repertoire of drills it uses each day aimed to accomplish fundamentals of blocking, ball handling, and movement.

During spring practice, offensive personnel, such as backs and interior linemen, spend more time working together in groups. Our inside attack in the inside drill and the half-line scrimmage is emphasized at this time. We also work our offensive personnel together so that we can develop some of our blocking techniques. For instance, our slotback might be with the ends, working on the double team block, or the ends and tackles might be together working on their double team block. On other occasions, we might have guards and centers working together on the trap technique.

Some of the basic fundamental skeleton drills (utilizing only a part of the offensive team) that are used include the: (1) inside drill, (2) outside drill, (3) half-line drill, (4) skeleton pass drill, (5) pass protection drill, and (6) Oklahoma drill.

(1) **Inside drill**—Personnel needed for the inside drill include the tackles, the guards, the center, and the backs. The drill is conducted by placing two dummies down on the ground just outside the offensive tackles; then by utilizing the backfield and the interior offensive line, the offense runs inside plays at an interior defense. (See Figure 2–10.) The offensive coaches are stationed so that each one can observe his respec-

tive personnel—the line coach observes the interior line and the back-field coach the backs.

This is a good drill that provides a game type environment and does a good job of preparing interior linemen to recognize different defenses and to execute proper play techniques. This drill also teaches the backs to recognize different defenses which will contribute to their anticipation of the area in which they should run the ball. This drill aids a back in learning to take the inside cut or the outside cut, when necessary, due to stunts by the defense. At the same time, coaches can observe individual players and note their aggressiveness, reaction, poise, effort, etc.

This drill serves as a good morale drill when a good offense is running against a defense of equal ability.

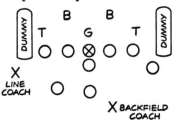

Figure 2–10. *The inside drill vs. the 5–2 defense.*

(2) Outside drill—The offensive players included in the outside drill are the tackles, the ends, and the backs. The drill is conducted by placing two dummies inside the offensive tackles, and then utilizing the tackles, the ends, and the backs to run off tackle and wide plays at a perimeter defense. (See Figure 2–11.)

The same benefits can be derived from this drill as from the inside drill. The only difference being the plays run.

Figure 2–11. *The outside drill vs. the loose tackle six defense.*

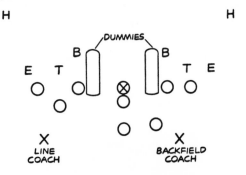

(3) **Half-line drill**—This drill includes the center and an entire side of the offensive line plus the backfield, and is designed so that the offense can work on a series of plays (for example, the split T series).

The drill is conducted by running one half of the offensive line plus the backs against one half of a certain defense. (See Figure 2–12.) Individual instruction is stressed and injuries are minimized.

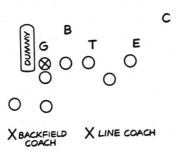

Figure 2–12. *The half-line drill vs. the 5–2 defense.*

(4) **Skeleton pass drill**—The skeleton pass drill utilizes the ends and backfield against a skeleton defense consisting of the corner defenders, the linebackers, and the secondary.

The passing period is spent working on both passing and receiving, but successful execution depends upon the passer and the receiver being able to recognize the defensive coverage and to attack it in its vulnerable areas.

If we are attacking an eight-man front with three-deep coverage, we must know if they play zone, man-for-man, or use calls to cover the flats, etc. Therefore, the defensive secondary that we would be throwing against would be set up during the pass period as in Figure 2–13.

Figure 2–13. *Skeleton pass drill vs. eight-man front three-deep secondary.*

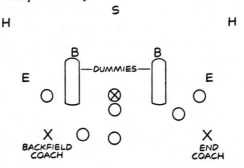

The blocking on the defensive ends should be "live" and the routes and coverage full speed. The prime consideration in the drill would be how different defensive coverages would be attacked, but no attempt will be made here to describe these operations since this will be covered in some detail in the chapter on the sprint out pass. (See Chapter 6, pages 141–176.)

Quarterbacks and receivers *must* learn to recognize the defensive alignment and learn to read the coverage on each and every play. This involves the corner defense, the linebacker coverage or blitz, and the secondary's zone, level off, or man coverage. Any defense can be attacked successfully when the passer and his receivers know the coverage, but the passing game will fail unless the offense can learn to *read* the defensive coverage.

If we are attacking a four-deep type of defense, the defense will be altered and an additional secondary defender added as seen in Figure 2–14.

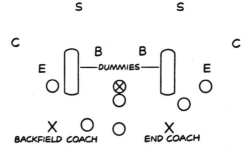

Figure 2–14. *Skeleton pass drill vs. seven-man front four-deep secondary.*

In addition to the protection and the reading of the particular coverage on a play, the final factor in the success of the passing game is that of proper timing. Timing is the most difficult single phase of the passing game. Much practice time must be allowed for the passers and receivers to become acquainted with each other's speed and moves.

Basically, in attacking a zone coverage, the passer and receiver not only must know, but also must anticipate the open area created by the particular pass route, and the ball must be delivered in the open area at the proper time. This may sound basic, but it is a must that the ball be delivered to the open area "on time."

In attacking man-for-man type coverage, the same basic idea exists, except that in this case success depends on an individual offensive receiver defeating an individual defensive man. The quarterback not only must know the offensive pass route and the receivers' moves, but, even more important, he must anticipate the cut in order for the ball to be delivered on the cut rather than after the receiver breaks open.

Perfecting the timing between the passer and the receiver is difficult but essential, since throwing "on time" is a key to success in any passing game.

In summary, the skeleton pass drill is designed for three major purposes:

(1) Protection
(2) Defensive recognition
(3) Timing

On particular practice days, the offensive guards will be added to the drill, in order to work on the bootleg passes with the same emphasis being placed on protection, defensive recognition, and timing as we have previously described in other drills.

(5) Pass protection drill—In the group work section of our football practice, we work on the individual pass protection techniques (this will be discussed in detail in the chapter on offensive line play) until we can execute them properly. (See Chapter 3.) After we accomplish our fundamentals relative to pass protection, we will work our interior offensive line as a unit against a scout team using the upcoming opposition defenses.

In this drill (see Figure 2–15), we will line up our offensive linemen, and the coach will call out a specific formation and pass play. On the snap count, the offensive linemen execute the proper protection techniques against the scout team that is rushing full speed or the dummy.

In the 10–15 minute pass protection period, a coach can check a complete pass protection plan against several defenses.

Figure 2-15. *The pass protection drill vs. the 5–2 defense.*

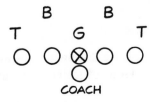

(6) Oklahoma drill—The Oklahoma drill should be used in practice when a coach wants to work offensive and defensive people in one-against-one situations in combination with backs carrying the ball. This drill is ideal for use early in spring practice when the team is building up to a full scrimmage. It can also be used when full-speed work is needed to regain form and technique, such as late in the football season when polishing up form is necessary.

One advantage of this drill is that it allows full-speed work with a minimum of people, and therefore cuts down on the chances of injury. Also it allows for concentrated teaching of the participants. It is also a good morale and pride drill as it pits one man against another when everyone is watching. Also, a coach can find out quickly where deficiencies in one-on-one blocking exist in his blocking front.

The Oklahoma drill is conducted in the following way: (See Figure 2–16.) A defender is placed between two large dummies which are placed 6 feet apart.

In front of the defender place a blocker. Behind the blocker place a back at normal depth with a ball. At the snap of the ball, the blocker lunges out and blocks the defender back and out from between the dummies and then turns him right or left. The back follows the blocker, runs between the bags, reads the direction of the block, cuts, and eludes the defender who is playing defense full speed.

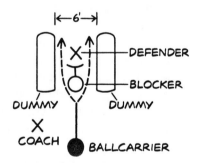

Figure 2–16. *Oklahoma drill.*

Teamwork

The final phase of the practice session is spent working the entire team as a unit. There are three levels of tempo that can be employed during teamwork depending on the needs of the offensive team: (1) dummy situation, (2) apron work, and (3) full-speed contact.

(1) Dummy situation—With only a few days left prior to game time, we will emphasize running the offensive team against a dummy defense. This dummy defense is put on by the freshman or "Scout" team. After the game plan has been prepared, a rehearsal of certain game situations is needed. The categories for these situations are: hash mark situations, middle of the field situations, short yardage situations, goal line and special play situations. The main aim of running against dummies is to ease off on contact to maintain timing and to concentrate on game plan execution.

(2) Aprons—Another method of working a whole offensive team in a manner that is not full-speed contact work and yet is not dummy would be by putting the defensive team in aprons.

Aprons are a form of padding (like a baseball catcher's chest protector) that straps on and covers a defender's legs, hips, and chest area. This padding restricts his movement and protects both the defender and the blocker; therefore, lessening the chances of injury to blocker and defender.

This type of teamwork is better for an offensive team than working against dummies because the defenders can react to the flow of the play and the offensive blocker can get a realistic picture of blocking real defenders.

Anytime during the football season that an offensive team needs full-speed work with restricted contact, it can be accomplished with a minimum of risk by their working against an apron team.

(3) Full-speed contact—Full-speed contact work is necessary in the spring training part of football when a coach is trying to find out who the better players are and is moving them from one position to another in order to develop the strongest possible team. Full-speed contact work is necessary in order to teach and properly evaluate personnel. In the spring, it is important to do some full-speed work virtually every day so that *all* players will get a thorough test.

In the fall, full-speed contact is kept to only that amount which is necessary to condition and sharpen up the offensive team. Once the desired levels of conditioning and timing have been achieved, full-speed contact work should be kept at a minimum so that the offensive team can concentrate on game preparation with a minimum of injuries.

Many factors determine the success or failure of a football team. This statement is true of the ball-control offensive team. However, the true key to offensive football success probably lies in the ability of the coaching staff to teach individual players to execute the offense properly.

Staff philosophy of the game will determine the type of offense, and practice time planning and organization will determine the methods used by the offense. But once these issues are decided, then comes the individual teaching and learning process. In the final analysis, the most important question is this: What kind of teaching job are the individual positional coaches doing with their players?

A willing player and an able, hard-working coach can accomplish much. Everyone in football knows that a good player must have speed, quickness, strength, and ability. But today, with many

3

Coaching the
Offensive Backs

good players, it should be a challenge to the coach to be the best teacher. The greatest satisfaction a coach can have is to see all of his players perform at the top level of their ability.

Every coach in football today will grade his players from film, etc., to determine their playing efficiency. It is important for a coach, particularly an assistant coach, to realize that the level of performance of his players is in reality a grade of the results of his teaching. A player's performance is the responsibility of the assistant coach and is the only true measure of the coach as a teacher.

In the final analysis, it is not how much a coach knows about the game of football but rather how effective he is in imparting this knowledge to his players, and then motivating them so that they will perform at the peak of their capabilities.

There are three basic segments of the offense: the backfield, the interior linemen, and the ends. The offensive coaching responsibilities are divided into these three major areas. In the following chapters, the techniques of play and the positional coaching methods and coaching points used by each will be discussed in some detail.

The Offensive Backs

Stance: The type of stance used by a back depends upon what position he is playing. Our slotbacks and tailbacks will use the same basic stance, while the fullbacks and the quarterbacks will use different types.

The slotback and tailback stance is a three-point stance comparable to a sprinter's stance in track. We like this stance because we want the backs in a position to explode on the snap of the ball. In this stance, the feet should be perpendicular to the line of scrimmage. The feet should be 1 to 2 feet apart and they should not be staggered more than toe to heel (see Figure 3–1).

Figure 3–1. *Position of feet in tailback's and slotback's stance.*

Best stance is toe-instep relationship of feet.

Tall players may have toe-heel relationship of feet in stance.

The weight on the feet should be equally distributed over the balls of the feet; and if the feet are turned out or turned in, more pressure will be placed on the inside or the outside of the foot leaving less surface to exert pressure on the initial movements. (See Figures 3–2 and 3–3.)

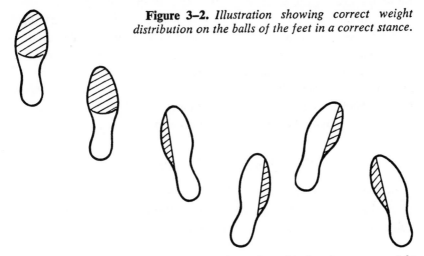

Figure 3–2. *Illustration showing correct weight distribution on the balls of the feet in a correct stance.*

Figure 3–3. *Illustration showing incorrect weight distribution on the balls of the feet in the stance.*

The hand that is placed down in the stance is placed on the ground in a position under the eyes and slightly inside the knee of the back foot. The elbow should be locked straight so that more weight can be shifted forward on the down hand. The fingers should be flexed in order to form a base of support. Enough weight should be shifted forward on the down hand to enable the back to really explode on his initial movement. The opposite arm should be rested on the thigh of the front leg. This arm should be bent and positioned just above the knee. The knees should be flexed at an angle that will keep the buttocks and hips high. The player's back should be straight and his shoulders should be parallel to the ground. A back's head should be tilted up slightly so that he can see ahead, and he should be looking in the vicinity of the heels of the offensive linemen.

The fullback's stance is different from the slotback's and tailback's stance in that his feet should not be staggered and he should not place much weight forward on the down hand.

This type of stance enables him to move laterally or forward equally well. Our fullback is called on to move laterally out of his stance on a substantial number of plays, and his stance must enable him to do this, losing neither motion nor time.

The desired position of the hands, the inclination of the body, and tilt of the head is the same as for the other deep back's stance.

The quarterback's stance is a two-point stance with the quarterback assuming a position that will enable him to move quickly. The quarterback's feet are spaced apart about the width of his hips and should be perpendicular to the line of scrimmage. The quarterback's knees should be bent and his back should be straight. The quarterback's head should be up, enabling him to look at the defense as he is calling the starting signals. His weight should be mostly on the balls of his feet.

The Offensive Back's Alignment

In our backfield we "flip-flop" our backs. The slotback will always be in the slot position, regardless of the offensive set, and the tailback will always be in the running back position.

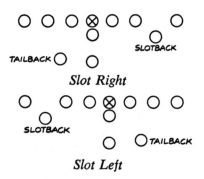

Figure 3–4. *The position of the slotback and the tailback in the tight slot sets.*

The alignment of the offensive backs in the tight slot formation is this: The tailback lines up 3½ yards from the line of scrimmage, splitting the outside foot of the offensive tackle. The fullback lines up 4½ yards from the line of scrimmage directly behind the center. The slotback lines up 1½ yards from the line of scrimmage and 1 yard outside the offensive tackle. The quarterback lines up under the center.

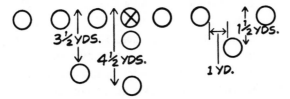

Figure 3–5. *The alignment of the offensive backs in the tight slot formation.*

The alignment of the offensive backs in the I-slot formation is this: The tailback lines up 5 yards from the line of scrimmage directly behind the center, quarterback, and fullback. The fullback lines up 3½ yards from the line of scrimmage, directly behind the center and quarterback. The slotback's alignment is the same as it is in the tight slot. The quarterback's alignment is always the same.

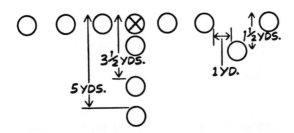

Figure 3–6. *The alignment of the offensive backs in the I-slot formation.*

In many situations, the offensive backs will adjust their alignment slightly in order to accomplish a certain objective. An example of this can be shown by illustrating our tailback's adjustment on the isolation play to the fullback (See Figure 3–7). On this play, we ask our tailback to move forward in his alignment ½ yard so that he is in a better position to attack the defensive linebacker, particularly if the linebacker is blitzing on the play.

Figure 3–7. *The adjusted alignment of the tailback on the isolation play to the fullback.*

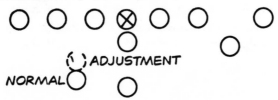

Moving on the Snap of the Ball

When the ball is snapped signaling the start of a play, each back should step correctly. This correct first step calls for him to step in the direction that he is going with his near foot while pushing off of the opposite foot. Backs should not use a crossover step unless the timing of the play necessitates this type of initial movement. The direction of the play will always direct the back's initial step. For example: On the split T option play to the right, the following should be the initial movement of all backs: The quarterback will step forward and laterally with his right foot, the fullback should step with his right foot parallel to the line of scrimmage and push off of his left foot, the slotback will step to the right with his right foot gaining depth and distance at the same time. The tailback will step forward with his back foot.

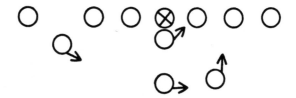

Figure 3–8. *First movement by the backs on the split T option play to the right.*

Offensive backs should attempt at all times to eliminate any loose movement that would cause them to slow down in getting to the point of attack. Once the correct first step is mastered then the correct movement of the body becomes easier.

The Center and Quarterback Exchange

There must be a proper exchange from the center to the quarterback for any offensive play to be successful. A large amount of time must be spent working on this technique.

The center should ask the official to rotate the ball so the laces are on the right side of the football as the center would look at the ball. Upon lining up, the center places his right hand (spread out) directly on top of the football with the top seam of the football being visible between the index and middle fingers. The center then tilts up the back end of the football (not more than 45 degrees) and places his left-hand, palm up, under the rear of the tilted ball. The ball is held so that it is perpendicular to the line of scrimmage, with the back end tilted up and held between the two hands. A moderate amount of body weight is shifted forward on the ball, and it is now in a position to be brought straight up between the center's legs (making a half turnover) and placed in the quarterback's hands with a swift pendulum swing of the center's right arm. The left hand is used to hold the ball firmly in the right hand, and the left hand leaves the ball halfway through the snap while the right hand completes it.

The position of the hands of the quarterback should be thumbs side by side with the hands spread out. The quarterback's hands press slightly forward in the natural curvature of the center's crotch, enabling the center to feel the position of the quarterback's hands.

Consistency and the elimination of exchange errors can best be accomplished with this type of snap.

Quarterback Techniques and Ball Handling in Ball-Control Offense

After the quarterback has taken the ball from the center, his job is just beginning. Whether it is a pass, handoff, lateral, or keep, he will begin the play. This is why we spend a great deal of time developing the techniques of quarterback play so we can try to eliminate mistakes such as the bad handoff, the fumble on the exchange from center, and interceptions.

Hands and Ball: The quarterback should have a firm grip on the ball with both hands. Once he has received the ball from the center, it should be brought into the abdominal section immediately. There should be no daylight between the ball and the stomach region.

There are many reasons why he should tuck the ball to his stomach as quickly as possible. First, defensive linemen will be slapping and grasping at the ball. Second, on quick fake and handoff plays the ball should be in front of the pocket formed by the player doing the faking because if contact with the ball is made by an elbow, a fumble could be the result.

One of our basic rules with the quarterback after he has received the ball from the center is to tuck it away or stomach it. This technique might seem fundamental but we feel fundamentals form the basic foundation of our team.

Movement of Hands: The quarterback's hands will be adjusted from time to time. The hands are adjusted to handoff, to faking, and to throwing the football.

Balance: Proper position of the quarterback's shoulders, hands, and arms is essential for proper execution of a play. We ask our quarterbacks to keep their weight on the balls of both feet until some movement is under way. Then the weight will be shifted according to the movement of the quarterback. On the reverse pivot, the quarterback's weight will shift toward the heel after he has pushed off the front part of his foot. We ask our quarterbacks to skip rope in order to help them develop spring and movement.

Spins and Pivots: When we spin out, we tell our quarterbacks to lift the heel of the stationary foot and pivot on the ball of the foot. This reverse movement begins with a push and circle motion of the body.

Half-Spins: The quarterback should open up quickly by pushing and stepping with the opposite foot, with the feet having a normal spacing between them.

Figure 3–9. *The quarterback's foot movement on a half-spin.*

Bootleg Technique: Whether it is used from a pivot movement or a front out, we want our quarterbacks to push off of the foot nearest the line of scrimmage and keep the feet well apart so that distance can be gained after push-off.

Figure 3–10. *The quarterback's foot movement on a bootleg action play.*

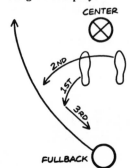

Sprint-Out: The weight should be equally distributed on both feet. Shift weight to the sprint-out side by pushing off the opposite foot and turning body slightly.

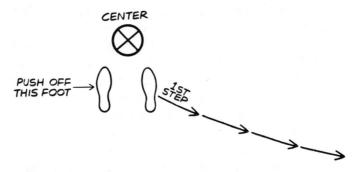

Figure 3–11. *The quarterback's foot movement on a sprint out play.*

The Faking Technique: Quite often our quarterbacks are called on to fake or ride with an offensive back and then pitch the ball or keep it. On such plays as the outside belly, inside belly, or bootlegs, we ask them to locate the pocket as soon as possible. Then the quarterback should put the ball in the pocket and position his body as close as possible to the faking back before the ball is withdrawn. The ball should be withdrawn as quickly as possible from the pocket after the back is even with, but not past, the quarterback. If a ride is desired, we want them to shuttle step, similar to a boxer's movement.

Figure 3–12. *Quarterback's shuttle step on the outside belly option play.*

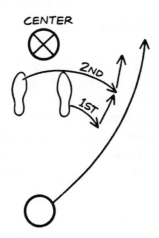

Forming Pockets: When taking a handoff, we ask our backs to create a pocket that is quite visible to our quarterback. When a back is taking a handoff, we want his near elbow high and extended with his thumb twisted slightly inward. The back's opposite hand should be close to his side in order to stop the ball from passing through the pocket and out the other side on the exchange. Once the ball is placed in the pocket, the ball should be grasped firmly by the back with both hands.

The Handoff: We tell our quarterbacks to give the ball to the runner; don't let him take it. We want the quarterback to assume the responsibility of the handoff unless the ball passes through the pocket and out the other side. First, the quarterback should find the target and concentrate only on locating the area for the exchange. The ball should be placed in the pocket with one hand. The type of exchange depends on the play being run. On the quick handoff play, we want our quarterback to place the ball into the pocket quickly and firmly.

On the fullback trap, we want the quarterback to place the ball in the pocket with a feather touch. After such handoffs, we expect the quarterback to assume the responsibility for recovering fumbles.

Blocking

The backs have very important blocking assignments. All backs should become proficient blockers. Blocking techniques are worked on every day during spring practice, and this drilling is continued throughout the season. The following is a list of blocks that we use:

1. Power Block.
2. Cut Block.
3. Post Drive.
4. Running Shoulder Block.
5. Pass Protection Block.

1. The power block—This block for our backs is basically the same as the one-on-one block used by the linemen. The best description of this block is actually found in the meaning of the words, power block —that is, to overpower your defensive opponent. We teach this to all of our backfield personnel, especially our slotbacks and fullbacks.

The essential coaching points are these: (1) keep eyes on target, (2) keep base low with feet spread apart, (3) make contact on the defender's belt buckle, (4) move upward after contact, (5) follow through with leg action.

This block is used on most inside plays, such as the power sweep or wedge.

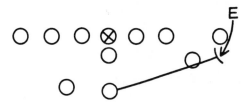

Figure 3–13. *The fullback power block on the defensive end on the off tackle power sweep.*

2. The cut block—The cut block is executed by our slotbacks, fullbacks, and tailbacks on plays designed to go wide.

The essential coaching points are these: (1) keep eyes on target, (2) dip beneath the defender's hands and make contact on the outside knee of the defender with the inside shoulder, (3) scramble defender's legs with both hands on the ground, (4) maintain body movement perpendicular to line of scrimmage, (5) follow through with leg action.

This blocking technique is used by our tailback in motion on the quarterback sprint keep play. His first responsibility would be to stop penetration by the defensive end. In order to do this, he must be aggressive. He must not hesitate to execute the cut-blocking technique described above.

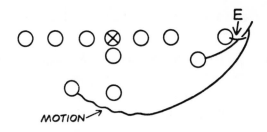

Figure 3–14. *The tailback's cut block on the quarterback sprint keep play.*

3. The post drive—This block is executed by our offensive end and slotback. If the slotback is to post, his concern is to stop penetration first; then execute a drive block. (This technique is described in Chapter 3.)

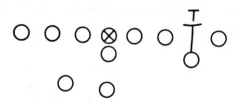

Figure 3–15. *The slotback's post drive block on the off tackle power sweep.*

4. The running shoulder block—This block is used most effectively on wide plays. Our fullbacks are drilled extensively on the proper execution of this block. The essential coaching points are these: (1) keep eyes on target, (2) maintain good balance, (3) establish speed, (4) duck head slightly, in order to get under the defensive player, before contact is made, (5) follow through with maximum momentum after initial contact, (6) never leave feet.

The plays that involve this type of block are mostly wide plays.

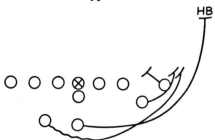

Figure 3–16. *The fullback's running shoulder block on the quarterback sprint out keep.*

5. The pass protection block—When protecting for the passer, our style of protection depends on the type of pass being thrown. When the play calls for pocket protection our fullback will step in the direction of the defensive end. (See Figure 3–17.)

Figure 3–17. *The fullback's pass protection block on the throwback pass.*

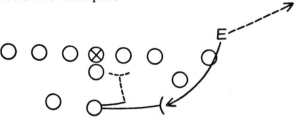

The essential coaching points are these:

1. The back must be aggressive and anticipate the defensive end crashing.
2. The back should keep buttocks low, before contact, and dip down by bending knees.
3. The back must explode with upward movement.
4. The back should carry defender in any direction that he commits.

If the defensive end drops off and becomes a pass defender, the fullback should turn immediately back to the inside and become a personal protector for the passer. The fullback's objective in case of this eventuality is to pick up any penetration possible.

Offensive Backfield Drills

Certain drills are used primarily to teach the offensive backs methods of evading tacklers as well as agility and quickness. These drills include the following ones: (See Figures 3–20 to 3–23) (1) the stiff-arm drill, (2) the spin drill, (3) the body control drill, and (4) the body balance drill.

(1) The stiff-arm drill—This drill is conducted by having two lines of backs face each other about 10 yards apart, with one line of men being stationary and having their hands on their knees. The other line, upon command, charges the stationary line and by using a right or left stiff-arm avoids the stationary line.

The coaching points of this drill are these: (1) the ballcarrier should start out at full speed and then come under control at 3 to 4 yards' distance from the defender, (2) the stiff-arm should be extended, with the elbow locked, straight toward the opponent's headgear where contact will be made, (3) the foot on the side of the cut should be planted and the other foot brought over in a crossover step as the opponent is pushed off, and (4) the ball should be carried under the arm opposite from the one doing the stiff-arming.

Figure 3–18. *The stiff-arm drill.*

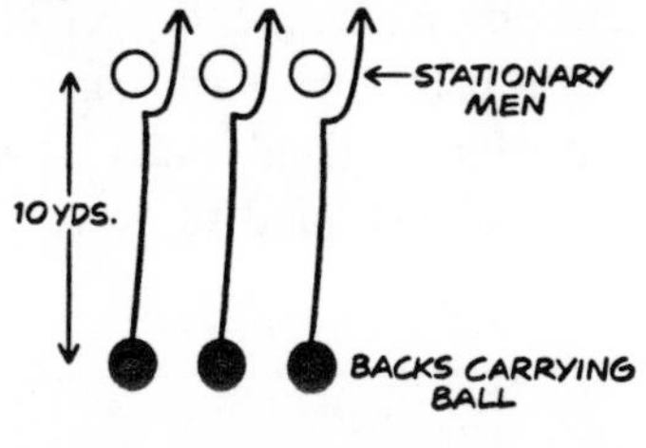

(2) The spin drill—The personnel alignment in the spin drill is identical to that used for the stiff-arm drill. (See Figure 3–18.) The drill is conducted in this manner: The ballcarrier charges full speed straight at the man in the stationary line and comes under control at about 3 or 4 yards distance from the opponent. Then he avoids the defender by using the stiff-arm technique while at the same time doing a 360 degree turn spinning to the side of the arm that is carrying the ball.

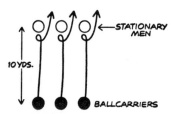

Figure 3–19. *The spin drill.*

(3) The body control drill—The personnel alignment in the body control drill is the same as that used in the stiff-arm and spin drills. This drill calls for the ballcarrier to charge full speed directly at the defender and to try to freeze him. Then by using a head fake, while under control and using short steps, the ballcarrier causes the defender to commit himself to one side or another while he breaks off and goes the opposite way.

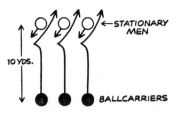

Figure 3–20. *The body control drill.*

(4) The body balance drill—The body balance drill is used to teach backs how to regain their body balance once they have lost it and are being forced to touch the ground with a hand in order to regain it.

The drill is conducted by forming a line of backs and having each one charge out carrying a ball. As a back charges, he reaches forward and touches the ground with his hand, palm down; then he pushes off the ground with the heel of his hand to regain his balance. He then changes the ball to the other arm and repeats the exercise pushing off with the opposite arm. The back should run forward about 10 to 15 yards while simultaneously alternating the exercise from left hand to right hand.

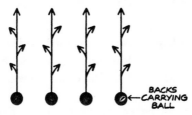

Figure 3-21. *The body balance drill.*

Other offensive backfield drills are used to teach backs how to run low and how to run viciously. These drills are designed to develop toughness and stamina in the offensive backs. These drills include the following ones: (1) the obstacle course drill, (2) the staggered bag obstacle course drill, and (3) the chute drill.

(1) The obstacle course drill—This drill is designed to teach offensive backs how to deliver a blow to a defender, with a forearm and a shoulder, and then release and continue on ahead to another defender where the same methods are used to evade him. This drill is conducted by having three men line up deep 3 or 4 yards apart, each holding a large dummy. Three or 4 yards from the end of and perpendicular to the dummy line, two men, each holding a large bag, stand 1 yard apart.

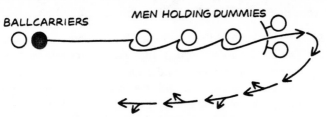

Figure 3-22. *The obstacle course drill.*

The coaching points for this drill are these:

(1) Have the back run full speed then come under control.
(2) The back should crouch and gather himself in order to deliver a forearm and shoulder blow.
(3) The back should explode into the bag, stay square, follow

through with leg action, then release and continue on to the next bag.

(4) The back should blast through the last two dummies and then return to the end of the line touching the ground with alternating hands while switching the ball from one hand to the other.

(2) The staggered bag obstacle course drill—This drill is designed to teach a back how to deliver a forearm and shoulder blow to one side and then, by quickly adjusting, how to deliver the same blow in close quarters to the opposite side.

In this drill, a line of backs will be facing four dummies which will be about 1½ yards apart and staggered. (See Figure 3–23.) Each back charges the first dummy and delivers a forearm and shoulder blow against it, releases, and strikes the second bag with the opposite forearm and shoulder; then he continues until the four dummies have been negotiated in this fashion.

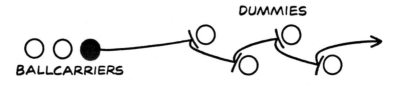

Figure 3–23. *The staggered bag obstacle course drill.*

The coaching points for this drill are these:

(1) The back should run full speed; then come under control.
(2) The back should crouch and gather himself, in order to deliver a forearm and shoulder blow.
(3) The back should step with his near foot at the dummy.
(4) The back should uncoil up through the dummy, release, adjust and step with the opposite foot, and deliver a blow from the alternate side at the next dummy.

(3) The chute drill—This drill is designed to teach backs how to run and how to fake by running low.

It is conducted by having an offensive back take a handoff or fake a handoff and then run through an 8-foot long, wire-covered tunnel that is 48 inches high. (See Figure 3–24.)

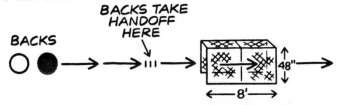

SIDE VIEW OF DRILL
Figure 3-24. *The chute drill.*

The coaching points for this drill are the following:

(1) The back should focus his eyes on the correct area.
(2) The back should form the correct pocket in order to take the handoff.

Blocking Drills

Blocking drills are used every day in order to develop the various components of the total blocking techniques and, second, to integrate these components into the total blocking techniques. Some of these drills include the following: (1) the punching drill, (2) the board drill, and (3) the technique drills.

(1) The punching drill—This drill serves to teach backs how to develop balance, proper foot movement, and the correct delivery of a shoulder blow.

This drill is conducted by having two defenders confront an offensive back whose job it is to block. (See Figure 3-25.) One defender should charge the back who delivers a blow upon him and resets himself ready to block again. Then the second player charges the back who turns, blocks him, and then resets himself. The first defender charges again, and the procedure is repeated.

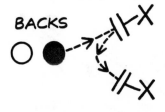

First defender charges then retreats to wait until second defender has charged; then he repeats charge

Second defender charges after first defender has charged, etc.

Figure 3-25. *The punching drill.*

The coaching points for this drill are the following:

(1) The blocker must stay low and move his feet.

(2) The blocker must step hard into the defender and then recover quickly ready to deliver another blow.

(2) The board drill—This blocking drill is used to teach backs proper one-on-one blocking form.

This blocking drill requires a board (10 feet long, 12 inches wide, and 2 inches thick, beveled on each side) and a large dummy which is held on one end of the board by a man. A back lines up in a normal stance in front of the dummy and, upon command, explodes into the dummy, using correct blocking form and follow-through, and drives the dummy down and off the end of the board. (See Figure 3–26.)

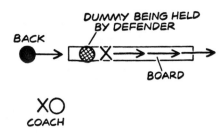

Figure 3–26. *The board drill.*

(3) The technique drills—In order to work on various blocking techniques, offensive backs can be lined up in their normal alignment and then can practice executing various techniques on dummies placed as linebackers, defensive ends, defensive halfbacks, etc. (See Figure 3–27.)

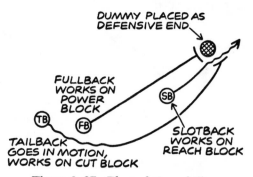

Figure 3–27. *The technique drills.*

Fumble Recovery Drill

Because of the ever-present danger of a fumble, offensive backs should be drilled often on fumble recovery. A simple drill that will teach backs the correct way to recover fumbles is this one: The offensive backfield coach stands in front of a line of backs, throws the ball on the ground, and checks the recovery technique. (See Figure 3–28.)

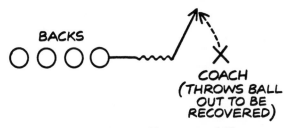

Figure 3–28. *Fumble recovery drill.*

The coaching point for this drill is the following:

(1) The back should go straight at the ball, grasp it with both hands, fall to the ground, and cover it with his body.

The Center-Quarterback Exchange Drill

A necessary drill for developing the proper center-quarterback exchange, it is conducted by having two or three centers snap the ball to two or three quarterbacks simultaneously. Action is initiated by having one of the quarterbacks give a starting count. By calling a certain play that requires certain quarterback action and having only one of the quarterbacks call the starting count, a coach can check the promptness of all of the centers' snaps and all of the quarterbacks' techniques. Any tardiness or slowness will be obvious to the coach as he watches the players perform together the same play on the same starting signal. (See Figure 3–29.)

Figure 3–29. *Center-quarterback exchange drill.*

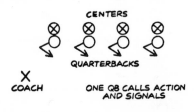

The coaching points for this drill are the following:

(1) The coach should call a certain play, thus designating the quarterback's action.

(2) The coach should then check the quarterback's steps, and ball-handling techniques.

Rushing the football is the heart of our offensive football system; therefore, we place great emphasis on the play of our offensive line and in the proper coaching of those points that produce sound blocking lines.

In coaching the offensive line, the coach must keep in mind the fact that, as a general rule, the offensive linemen often do not get as much recognition as other team members get. Consequently, offensive linemen could feel that their jobs are not important ones. The wise coach sells his men on the importance of the offensive line, and he sees that they are properly recognized for good work. This promotion helps to remove the "thankless job" stigma that can be troublesome.

In order to be a good offensive lineman, a player needs size, strength, and quickness, because much of line play is simply one man trying to defeat another. Good offensive linemen must have a capacity for conditioning and stamina that

4

Coaching the
Offensive Line

will enable them to establish superiority over a defender late in a football game.

It is good to try to fit certain men with specific physical qualities into the interior offensive line positions.

At offensive tackle, we like to put our biggest, strongest, and most experienced linemen. We play against odd defensive fronts a great deal, and we require our tackles to block the defensive tackle one-on-one. Therefore he needs to be physically equipped.

At offensive guard, we place quick linemen. The offensive guards must be able to help the double team block, they must be able to cut off linebackers, and they must be able to pull and lead the blocking on certain wide plays.

We place a quick man at offensive center. The center must be able to cut off linebackers and he must be able to handle the middle guard in an odd defense.

Offensive line play is divided into three major areas:

(1) The offensive lineman's stance and start.
(2) The offensive lineman's ability to identify and recognize defenses.
(3) The offensive lineman's ability to perform techniques.

(1) *The Offensive Lineman's Stance and Start*

A. Stance: We begin all of our offensive plays by lining up in a stance. Therefore, we must use a stance that is comfortable and yet one that will enable our linemen to accomplish their goals. Also, the stance has to be one that can be used on every type of play so that our linemen won't be telling the defense what blocking technique they plan to use.

The stance that we strive for is this: A three-point stance with one foot slightly ahead of the other. The feet should be shoulder width apart. The hand on the side of the back foot should be down and it should touch the ground directly under the eyes. Having the hand touch the ground directly under the eyes enables the offensive lineman to glance in at the rear of the football and line up close to the ball, but not offside.

COACHING TIPS: Be sure that the toe of the back foot is not any further back than the instep of the front foot and that both feet point straight ahead. This facilitates lateral movement, pulls, etc. and makes possible short steps on forward movement. The body weight should be mostly on the balls of the feet with a slight amount placed forward on the down hand. The player's back should be parallel to the ground. The knees should be slightly closer together than the feet. The off forearm should be relaxed and rested on the front knee. Both shoulders should be the same distance from the ground. The lineman's head is slightly up, but the neck should be relaxed, and he sees by looking ahead with his eyes up as if to look through his eyebrows.

The teaching of proper offensive stance takes deliberate work and time. We emphasize the stance early in spring practice during teaching periods both in the classroom and on the field. We describe and demonstrate our stance and cover the coaching points over and over again so that our men can coach themselves and help each other. On the field in our specialty period, we line up our first five interior linemen in an offensive stance. We will then check and correct their form while the other linemen watch and listen. Then we take the second five linemen and repeat the procedure. In a few minutes each man in the group will get several repetitions. Throughout all of our drills—individual, group, and team—we work to improve on our stance.

B. Starts: A good offensive line must move simultaneously and explosively *as a unit* on the snap of the ball. This type of coordination and effort requires much concentration and discipline on the part of the offensive linemen. Time should be set aside each day in which the offensive line (entire team is preferable) can work as a unit with stance and starting as the main objective.

We like our men to use these techniques on a straight-ahead movement from the line of scrimmage: (1) Lunge outward (but not upward). (2) Lock the head up between the shoulders, arch the back and dip the buttocks, and after full body weight is well ahead of the feet take a short step (1 to 1½ feet) with the back foot and roll off the ball of the front foot. After this initial lunge and following step, the lineman should continue with short steps in which the feet are kept shoulder-width apart. After the first two steps, the lineman should begin to drive upward with the blocking surfaces in order to get lift and to maintain balance.

The drill that we use to emphasize stance and starting is our 2–S drill (stance and starts). We use it as a team drill early in each practice with the main objectives being correct offensive stance and an explosive start. For explanations and diagrams of the 2–S drill, see Chapter 2, page 35.

(2) *The Offensive Lineman's Ability to Recognize and Identify Defenses*

A good offense is based on the principle of eliminating as many mistakes as possible: fumbles, interceptions, penalties, and missed blocking assignments. It does not matter how well an offensive line can block; if they are not blocking the correct defender, the play will fail.

We use 0, 1, 2, 3, 4 type blocking. The center might have these rules on certain plays, for example: (A) Drive 0, no one there—block offside linebacker; or (B) Drive 0, no one there—lead on No. 1 on the onside. The guards, tackles, and ends have similar rules; therefore, our linemen must be able to recognize defensive alignments and be able to number the defenders, thus enabling them to apply their blocking rule.

We start out numbering the defense in this manner: The defender over the center is 0 if there is one. The first man on either side is 1, the second man to either side is 2, third man is 3, and the fourth man is 4.

For a complete discussion of and illustrations of the numbering of the various defenses, see Chapter 1, Figures 1–2 through 1–11.

Once offensive linemen have learned to recognize various defenses and can identify the 0, 1, 2, 3, and 4 men in them, the team can have sound blocking regardless of what defense the opposition might use.

In the fall in preparation for each game, we take all the defenses that our opponents might use and go over the correct identification of each defender. We do this first on the meeting room blackboard and then again in a teaching period on the field using a demonstration team. Repetition is the key in learning to recognize and identify defenses.

COACHING TIPS: Drill (See Figure 4–1). Have offensive linemen sit in chairs in their regular offensive positions. Place a defensive team in front of them and have the defensive team line up in the opposition's various defenses. Call out a play and have the offensive linemen point out their assignments by number; 0, 1, 2, 3, and 4. In a short time, an entire offensive game plan can be checked against several defenses.

Figure 4–1. *Defense identification drill.*

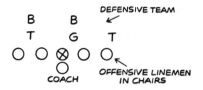

As an additional aid in teaching correct assignments, a coach should draw up the blocking assignments against the opposition's defense before each game, and he should give them out to his players for them to study during free time.

(3) *The Offensive Lineman's Ability to Perform Techniques*

The Offensive Center: One of the most important responsibilities on our offensive team, and one that is often taken for granted, is the center's first job—snapping the ball.

Regardless of whether he is fresh or tired, whether the ball is wet or dry, whether it is hot or cold, the center must snap the ball flawlessly and on time if a team is to have a smooth, well-timed offense. After this primary responsibility has been fulfilled, the center becomes a key offensive lineman in that he is never far from the point of attack and must be a good blocker.

In addition to snapping the ball to the quarterback and being a good blocker, the center has to master the long snaps—those for extra points, field goals, and for punts; and these techniques must be near perfection.

Our center also has the responsibility of setting our offensive huddle 6 yards from the ball on every play and getting everyone to hustle to the huddle to get the play.

All in all, being a center takes a special kind of athlete. He has to be a leader. He has to be consistent, and above all he has to be willing to sacrifice and work hard before and after practice in order to develop the various snapping techniques.

It is no small wonder that for two of the past four years one of our team captains has been our center.

Center's Stance: Our center's stance is very similar to our offensive lineman's stance, but modified so that he can snap the ball. We want his feet slightly wider than his shoulders and perpendicular to the line of scrimmage. Both feet should point straight ahead. The center's knees should be slightly bent with most of his body weight on the balls of his feet and a moderate amount placed forward on the ball. The center's shoulders should be parallel to the ground and his head held up, out the neck should be relaxed. He sees ahead by looking forward with his eyes through this eyebrows. His back should be parallel to the ground.

The Snap Technique: The center-quarterback exchange is discussed in detail in Chapter 3, page 50.

The long snap technique that we teach has room for individual differences and preferences. We want the center to hold the ball well out in front of himself with the throwing hand rolled well under the front of the ball and the other hand placed on top of the ball to hold it firmly in the throwing hand and to add impetus to the snap. When working on long snaps, a center should always ask for and snap to a definite target—the hands of the holder or punter. After a long snap, the center must discipline himself to raise up quickly and brace himself in order to become a blocker.

Drills: For initial work on the center-quarterback exchange, we have the center assume an offensive stance ready to snap and a quarterback line up ready to take the ball from him. The center snaps the ball into the quarterback's hands at half speed and, without releasing the ball, brings it back into his starting stance. By doing this over and over he soon gets the "feel" of the quarterback's hands and the proper snap technique. Once the center has the proper form, we use another drill to further polish the exchange. In this drill, the quarterback and center line up, the quarterback calls a play, takes the snap and reverses out or fronts out (depending on the play called), while the center snaps the ball and takes a short step with the proper foot. This drill helps to develop the confidence and smoothness necessary for the center-quarterback exchange.

Our centers work daily in specialty periods, snapping to the holders and punters in kicking drills. We do this so the centers, punters, and holders will develop a mutual "feel" for each other in this phase of the kicking game. In the spring, and in the fall, centers often remain after practice to work on long snaps until such time as they have this specialty polished. In all extra practice work, it is important that they give full concentration and effort to what they are doing in order to improve their technique.

The One-on-One Blocks: Offensive line play is the very foundation of offensive football. This means having to master many blocking techniques and being efficient in their execution.

The most important skills for an offensive lineman to master are the one-on-one blocking techniques. Whether it is a pass protection technique, a trap technique, or a straight-ahead type technique, we still think of it as one-on-one blocking. Because of the importance of these techniques to the success of our type of offense, we spend a great amount of time and use a wide variety of drills in each practice to develop a high level of proficiency in one-on-one blocking techniques.

We use six types of close, line, one-on-one blocks: (1) Drive, (2) Reach, (3) Reverse shoulder, (4) Trap, (5) Cutoff, and (6) Gap.

Drive Block

To our way of thinking, the straight ahead or drive block is the most important one that we use. A drive block is an uncomplicated block that allows us to line up, explode out, and defeat a defender by sheer quickness and aggressiveness with a minimum of finesse. It is a block that less talented boys may become adequate in executing. Also, the drive block is one in which our linemen can develop a sense of "pride," an ingredient they must possess in large quantity in order for us to be successful. Another important aspect we recognize is that good drive blocking techniques and pride carry over into the proper execution of other types of blocks requiring more talent and discipline.

For ease in teaching and coaching, we break down our drive block into four steps: (a) start, (b) contact, (c) lift, and (d) follow-through.

(a) Start—Our start is covered in detail in the section on stance and starts, but the main points should be restated. The blocker must lunge outward with all his body weight directly behind his helmet and shoulder pads. As he starts, he locks his head up between his shoulders and he looks directly at the target (we use the defender's belt buckle as the target). As he lunges, rolling off the ball of the front foot and stepping with his back foot, he arches his back. (When a defender is inside or outside the blocker we step with our *near* foot.) At this point the blocker's weight is well ahead of his feet.

(b) Contact—Contact must be made with the defender at a point below his protection (hands, forearm, shoulders) and in the middle of his body. The blocker should be head-on at contact and blocks *through* the defender. His tail should be kept low and his knees should be close to the ground to create a slight lifting action at contact. Initial velocity and leg drive will stop the defender and knock him off balance.

(c) Lift—After initial contact has been made and the defender has been knocked off balance, the blocking surfaces should be driven upward and the head slid off the belt buckle and by the defender's hip. The knees and tail should be kept low in order to get the best possible lifting action.

(d) **Follow-through**—Once the blocker has the defender stopped and off balance he should pinch the defender between his shoulder and forearm and his helmet. The blocker's weight is still tight against the defender, and he "runs" the defender backward with short, wide, quick steps. If the defender recovers and threatens to get away, the blocker should slide his head and shoulders by the defender's legs and then use a scrambling, high, four-point, crab-type block to screen him out of the pursuit.

Blocking Drills: It is important for us to start slowly in teaching drive blocking. Many boys have never used the technique that we use, putting their forehead on the target at contact, and if we had them do this full speed in the beginning before they had a chance to develop confidence and form, we would ruin some good linemen.

At the beginning of spring practice we start out with drills designed to teach parts of the total drive block technique. Usually, sleds and dummies are utilized in these drills. As our men progress, we graduate to drills where we use the total technique against men in aprons. Having mastered these drills, we move on to full-speed game situation drills. Regardless of how much progress we feel that we have made in our blocking, we will still use fundamental type drills every day in spring and fall practice.

The following drills are used to teach drive blocking:

2 Man Crowther Sled Drills

1. Hit! Hit! Hit! Drill: In this drill we place a man on a crowther sled to make it more difficult to move.

Two linemen assume an offensive stance in front of the sled. Upon the command "Hit!" they explode out against the sled without bringing up their feet and then as quickly as possible resume their correct offensive stance ready for the next two commands. (The second and third "Hit!") After the third explosion, we have our linemen do a seat roll to the outside, come up on their feet quickly, and sprint ahead for 5 yards. We want the linemen to hold their heads up as they drive them by the edge of the sled pads while looking ahead. Their backs should be arched and their tails and knees low. The men strive for full extension of their bodies while blasting the sled as hard as possible.

The purpose of this drill is to develop initial velocity and striking power to go with correct stance and blocking form.

2. Hit and Drive Drill: We place a man on a sled so that: (1) the sled will resist being moved, (2) the sled will push back hard when the blockers make initial contact.

Two men assume an offensive stance. Upon command they execute an initial lunge into the sled, immediately bring their feet up under them, and begin driving the sled using short, wide, quick steps in order to sustain the block. In this drill, we strive for a smooth and accelerated transition from the initial lunge into the lift and drive part of the block. In all of our hit and drive drills, we emphasize that we really are "blocking with our legs."

3. Board Drills with Dummies: We use boards and dummies for drive blocking drills in order to teach the blocker to keep a wide base, have greater initial exertion, and maintain better balance than in two-man sled drills.

The drill that we probably use most is a simple one in which we take a board (12 feet long, 10 inches wide, and 2 inches thick) and place a man with a large, heavy dummy on one end. (See Figure 4–2.) The blocker lines up in front of the board and dummy and, upon command, explodes out into the center of the dummy. He starts the dummy backward, slides his head to one side, straddles the board, and, using lift and short, wide, quick steps, drives the dummy down and off the board. We demand maximum exertion from the blocker all the way through this drill. Only by always pushing against his own physical limit can a blocker hope to expand that limit and thus be a better blocker.

Figure 4–2. *The one-on-one board drill.*

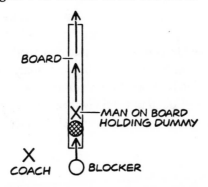

A variation of the above drill that we use and like requires the same setup with the only difference being that the man holding the dummy is about 2 yards from the end of the board. (See Figure 4–3.)

The blocker assumes a stance and upon command fires out, moves the 2 yards before he makes contact, and blocks the dummy off the end of the board.

This drill simulates a drive block in which the blocker must move a couple of yards before contact is made. Blocks against linebackers and various trap techniques require this. We are trying to teach the blocker to run through the defender without "staggering" upon contact. The same start, contact, lift, and follow-through is required for this type of block.

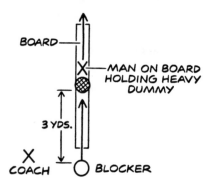

Figure 4–3. *The one-on-one linebacker drill.*

Board Drill Using a Man in Aprons: As we improve in our board drills with the dummies, we will start blocking live defenders. The first drill we use that is man vs. man requires the same setup as the first board drill mentioned (see Figure 4–3) except that we replace the dummy on the board with a man in protective aprons. (This is to protect the blocker as well as the defender.)

The procedure for the drill is the same as mentioned in Figure 4–2. In this drill, a young blocker can get the feel of blocking a man.

Full-Speed One-On-One Drill (Oklahoma Drill): This is a drill that we use after we are satisfied that our linemen understand and can execute the basic fundamentals of the drive block against the sleds and dummies.

We take two large dummies and lay them down parallel 2 yards apart. We place a defender in the desired defensive stance (down for defensive linemen, up for linebackers) between the dummies, and place an offensive lineman in front of the defender. A ballcarrier is lined up behind the offensive linemen and is instructed to run between the dummies. The coach stands behind the defender and signals to the blocker the count and the side to which he wants the blocker to slide his head. (See Figure 4–4.) On the snap, the blocker lunges out and executes a drive block on the defender and blocks him back and out from between the dummies. The ballcarrier runs between the dummies, and the defender tackles him if he has not been blocked.

This is a very competitive drill which simulates game type conditions. Properly done, it lets the coach know quickly where deficiencies in drive blocking techniques exist.

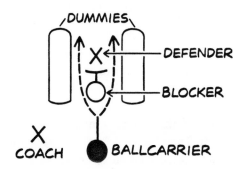

Figure 4–4. *The one-on-one drill (Oklahoma drill).*

These are some of the drive blocking drills that we have used. Our staff is always looking for ways to improve our drills. We want to keep them as varied as possible, always keeping in mind what improvements we are striving for and what game situations we are trying to simulate.

The Reach Block

The reach block is a technique that we would use when an offensive lineman has to block a defender who is lined up between him and the point of attack. He must "reach" out and block him, preferably off the line of scrimmage and if at all possible to the inside.

In the sprint action pass (see Figure 4–5), the right guard and tackle have reach blocking techniques to execute.

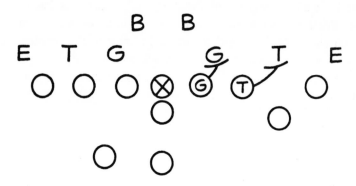

Figure 4–5. *The reach blocks by the offensive guard and tackle on the sprint action pass.*

At the University of Georgia, we teach the blocker to step with his near foot directly at the outside hip of the defender and then execute a drive block. He should be low and must drive his helmet tight across the belt buckle of the defender to his outside hip. The defender is knocked off balance and the blocker pinches him between his helmet, shoulder, and forearm. The blocker drives straight through the defender, and once he gets him started backward, he begins to work around him trying to get his body between the defender and the point of attack.

COACHING POINTS: The blocker must step directly at the defender and not try to position step: (1) in order to protect against the defender slanting to the inside, and (2) to get to him as quickly as possible. Staying low and getting to the defender quickly is the key to the block.

The Reach Blocking Drill: To work on reach blocking, we use this drill: A defender is dressed in aprons and lined up outside an offensive lineman, simulating a game situation. A ballcarrier is placed behind the blocker with instructions to run wide. (See Figure 4–6.) On the snap, the offensive lineman executes a reach block on the defender who plays the blocker and tries to pursue the ballcarrier.

The defender must play the blocker first and then pursue the ball-carrier (though slowed by the aprons) in order for the drill to work. The blocker should try to work around the defender, but if he can't, he stays with him and takes him anywhere that he can. The important thing is for him to *stay after the defender.*

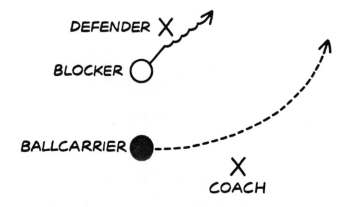

Figure 4–6. *Reach block drill.*

The Reverse Shoulder Block

Our interior linemen use this blocking technique on plays where we are using misdirection action in the backfield. That is, we are faking a run to one side and running to the other.

To execute this technique properly, the offensive lineman must lunge out at the defender butting him on the belt buckle. At this time, the fake in the backfield will draw a reaction and a movement from the defender toward the fake. As the defender moves toward the fake, the blocker slides his head off the belt buckle to a position between the defender and the fake. At the same time, he brings up his off shoulder and forearm high and hard into the defender, pinching him between the blocking surfaces and the head. From this point, the lift and follow-through are the same as for the drive block.

Drill: In our reverse shoulder blocking drill, we place an offensive blocker in his stance with a defender lined up head on. On the snap, the blocker lunges out and butts the defender on the belt buckle. At this time, the coach who is standing directly behind the blocker steps right or left and the defender (who is told to react in the direction that the coach steps) pursues. With the reaction of the defender, the blocker executes the reverse shoulder blocking technique.

Figure 4–7 *Reverse shoulder block drill.*

Trap Blocking

We use both guards and both tackles to trap with in our defense. Usually our guards execute the quick-hitting, short trap techniques on plays such as the fullback trap up the middle or off tackle. Our tackles will trap on misdirection type plays or long counter traps.

To execute a proper trap technique, an offensive lineman must start from a neutral stance (little stagger in feet and slight amount of weight on down hand). Upon the snap, the blocker looks at the inside hip of the defender that he will trap and takes a short step with his near foot directly at that point. Without raising up, the blocker brings up his off foot and is now facing the defender. From this point the blocker executes a running drive block upon the defender (see drive-block board and dummy drills), driving straight through his inside hip.

COACHING POINTS: The blocker must explode through the defender and move him quickly in order not to get in the ballcarrier's way.

Trapping linemen must keep an inside-out angle on the defender in order to make the block. (See Figure 4–8.)

Figure 4–8. *Illustration showing correct trap angle for pulling guards.*

In this diagram the pulling guard swings too deep and loses his blocking angle.

In this diagram the pulling guard steps directly at the defender keeping a good inside-out blocking angle.

If the defender charges hard straight ahead and crosses the line of scrimmage, the trapping lineman should butt him on his inside hip, slide his head off in front of him, and use a reverse shoulder block, driving him out. When the defender slants hard to the inside or closes down, the blocker should butt him on his belt buckle and use a reverse shoulder block, driving him to the inside or straight upfield.

Drill: In addition to the hit and drive drills that constitute part of the trapping technique, we use the following drills to coordinate the total trap technique. (See Figure 4–9.) Because of the timing and coordination necessary on this type of play, we work with most of or all of our interior line in these drills.

Figure 4–9. *Drill to develop trap blocking.*

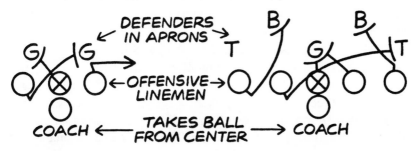

Trap vs. Even Defense   *Trap vs. Odd Defense*

Cutoff Block

This is the technique that our linemen use to wall off a defender and keep him out of the pursuit. We like to use this block when it is not necessary to "drive" the defender, only screen him. For example, the center's technique on a soft-playing middle guard on a wide sweep would be to use a cutoff block.

In this technique, we want the offensive player to lunge out as if to drive-block the defender; but instead, at the last moment, we want him to drive his arm and shoulder outside of and on by the defender's knee without making contact with his own arm or shoulder. From this point the blocker will go into a high, four-point crab block and actually try to scramble around the defender, making him take an inside release. (See Figure 4–10.)

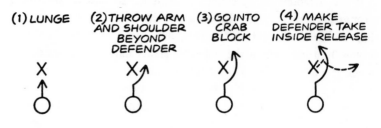

Figure 4–10

COACHING TIPS: The blocker must get as close as possible to the defender before he throws his arm and shoulder on by his knee. Also, the blocker must throw the block at a spot about 1 yard behind the defender and then quickly begin to crab on around him. As the blocker's arm and shoulder is slid by the defender's knee, the blocker should bring his inside knee up against the defender's legs, and he should pinch them between his arm and leg as he scrambles the defender.

Drill: A simple drill to use when work on the cutoff block is needed is this one: (See Figure 4–11.) Place a defender in the desired defensive position (down, up, close, off the ball, etc.) in front of an offensive lineman. Behind the blocker, place a ballcarrier. The coach should stand behind the defender to signal the blocker which way he wants him to go to cut off the defender. The ballcarrier should run the ball to that same side also. The defender tries to pursue and tackle the ballcarrier while the blocker executes the proper cutoff technique.

Figure 4–11. *The cutoff block drill.*

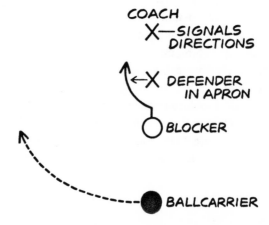

The Gap Block

In situations where the defender is lined up in a gap and is trying to penetrate the line of scrimmage, we think that the normal drive block technique is too risky to use in blocking such a man because of the possibility of missing him. We use instead a technique called a gap block on a defender using this type charge.

To properly execute this technique, the blocker must step at the defender with his near foot and the blocker must drive his head tight across the belt buckle in *front* of the charging defender, then he must use proper lift and follow-through. This block is much like the reverse shoulder block with the difference being that the blocker immediately drives his head in front of the defender to seal off his penetration.

COACHING TIPS: If the defender is charging quickly, the blocker must anticipate this and allow for it by leading the defender. That is, aim slightly ahead of him as he steps to block him.

Against a man using a gap charge, an offensive lineman should cut down on his split in order to limit the area that the defender can charge through.

The Double Team Block

In our offensive blocking scheme, we double team men playing head on (a middle guard over the center) and we double team men in gaps (stack type defenses). The fundamentals and the goals in double teaming these types of defenders are basically the same. We want the man blocked straight off the line of scrimmage in order: (1) to move him, and (2) to wall off pursuit. We intend to make our running room behind the double team block, and our linemen know this.

To properly double team a defender, the offensive linemen must first take a proper split. This means not being so far apart that they cannot get the job done, and yet not so close that the defender knows that a double team is coming.

We tell our linemen that a double team is actually a double-drive block. At the snap, both blockers lunge out aiming directly at a point 2 inches inside the near hip of the defender while stepping with their near foot.

Since both blockers step with their near foot, they come closer together. They should continue to work their inside hips toward each other. Working toward each other takes a conscious effort as there is a natural tendency to "split" when contact is made with the defender.

After initial contact, both men should slide off into drive blocks. The blockers should execute the proper lift and follow-through technique, and they should drive the defender straight up the field.

The onside blocker in the double team is responsible for containing the defender in case he recovers and tries to roll toward the ballcarrier.

Drill: (See Figure 4–12.) In our drill for the double team block, we place the two offensive linemen who will have to execute this block in their respective offensive stances. (*Example:* Center and guard or guard and tackle.) On defense, in aprons, we place a defender in the proper position (head up on one of them, in the gap, etc.). On the snap, they execute the double team block with the defender fighting to defeat it. Initial lunge, staying low, staying together, and powerful leg-drive are the key ingredients in double team blocking.

Figure 4–12. *The double team blocking drill.*

Downfield Blocking

Our offensive tackles' downfield blocking technique is the same one that is used by our offensive ends. For a discussion and explanation of this type of block, see Chapter 5, page 125.

Pass Protection Blocking

At Georgia, we use two types of pass protection: play action and throwback. Basically our play action passes call for aggressive type blocking, and our throwback passes call for drop-back protection techniques. At times we will use combinations of aggressive and drop-back blocking techniques on both types of passes against certain defenses in order to get the best protection.

Play Action Pass Protection

We have two categories of play action pass protection. They are: (A) bootleg protection and (B) regular play pass protection.

(A) Bootleg Protection: Bootleg pass protection is called for when we have faked a run to one side and then brought the ball back to the other side to throw. In this protection scheme, we will pull the offside guard to block on the corner, and we will block aggressively all along the blocking front in order to simulate a run as much as possible. For bootleg pass blocking rules and pass patterns, see Chapter 6, pages 144–145.

Bootleg protection drills: The reach and drive techniques called for in certain of the bootleg pass blocking rules have already been described in the section on one-on-one blocking techniques. There are two new techniques required that we have not described previously. They are: (1) drop-stepping to protect an area and (2) the pulling and blocking technique used by the offside guard.

(1) Drop-stepping—This technique is used when a blocker might not have a defender to drive block and thus is called upon to protect an area. In the following play diagram (see Figure 4–13), the onside guard will drop-step with his right foot and block anyone coming into the area between the center and the onside tackle.

Figure 4–13. *Drop-step used by the onside guard when his blocking assignment (#1) retreats to play pass defense.*

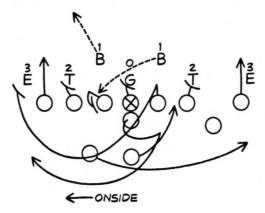

←—ONSIDE

Drill for drop-stepping technique: To drill guards or tackles (both have to perform this move) in drop-stepping, place a blocker in an offensive stance and line up a defender 2½ to 3 yards in front of him. A coach will then stand behind the blocker and signal the defender to rush or retreat. If he rushes, the blocker is to step to the onside and then execute a drive block upon him. If the defender retreats, the blocker should step to the onside and then drop-step with his inside foot and hold his position ready to block any other defender coming into his area. (See Figure 4–14.)

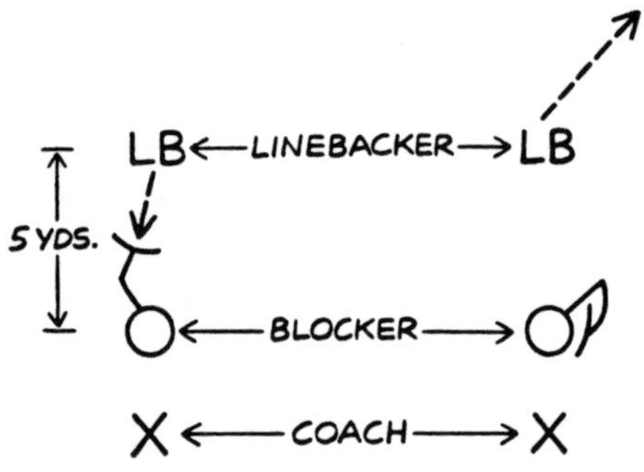

Blocker steps. Linebacker rushes.   Blocker steps. Linebacker retreats.
Blocker executes drive block.   Blocker drop-steps and protects area.

Figure 4–14. *Drill for drop-stepping techniques for guards.*

(2) Pulling guard technique—From a neutral stance, the guard takes a short forward step with his outside foot, pivots, and pulls back at a 45 degree angle sprinting to get 4 yards behind the line of scrimmage. He continues sprinting in a circular arc aiming to block the outside hip of the first man outside the offensive end.

On the first backward step at the beginning of his pull, the guard must find the defender he is to block and see him all the way until he blocks him. His blocking technique is a drive block on the outside hip of the defender.

Drill: Have a guard assume an offensive stance and place a stand-up dummy in the proper defensive position (at defensive end). Have the guard step up, pull at the proper angle, get the desired depth, sprint the correct arc, and then execute a drive block on the dummy.

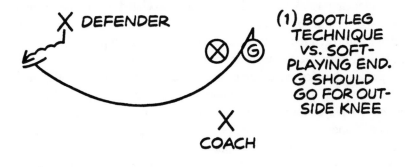

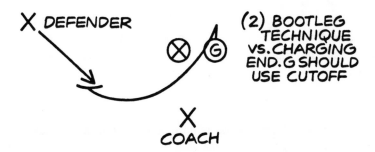

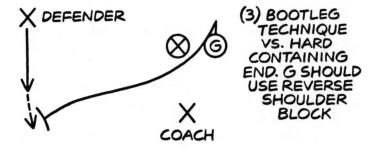

Figure 4–15. *Bootleg pulling drill for offensive guards.*

(B) Regular Play Action Pass Protection: We use regular play action pass protection when a run is faked to one side and the ball is thrown from that same side.

For blocking rules and pass patterns associated with play action passes, see Chapter 6, pages 146–147. On regular play pass protection, the drive and reach techniques and the drop-step techniques called for in the blocking rules are the same as for bootleg protection.

In preparation for each game, our coaches set up our bootleg and regular play pass protection in advance of player meetings and actual practice. At player meetings, we review our protection schemes on the blackboard and then have a walk-through session on the practice field, using a team to demonstrate the opposition's defenses.

Later in group work, we might work on various protection techniques "full speed" in order to improve them. For example, we might practice the guards' pulling techniques, the reach blocks, the drop-step, and area protection techniques.

In our team passing period, we will put the protection techniques together and protect the passer full speed as a team, until we feel that we have had the rough work that is necessary to coordinate our total protection.

Throwback Protection

Our throwback pass series requires our quarterback to take the ball and start out as if to sprint wide with the quarterback run or throw play, but instead he will pull up and throw from a position about 6 or 7 yards behind our offensive tackles. Therefore, our throwback protection is designed to protect an area 5 to 7 yards directly behind one of our offensive tackles.

In this scheme of pass protection, we do not block aggressively. Instead, our blockers will step to the onside for position and then execute a drop-back type protection technique on the defenders as they rush the passer.

This protection plan is "area" pass protection, because we designate a certain area to be blocked by each offensive blocker rather than blocking "man" for the protection of the passer.

For blocking rules and pass patterns associated with throwback passes, see Chapter 6, page 169.

In our throwback protection, the line blocking techniques are different from other protection techniques already described in that we want our lineman to jab-step quickly to the onside and slightly forward remaining low, and then drop back about 1 yard placing himself directly between his man and the passer, staying low and ready to block.

As the defender comes toward the offensive lineman, the blocker holds his ground moving his feet as if running in place but keeping them shoulder width apart. When the rusher is about to make contact with the blocker, the blocker lunges up at the rusher butting him in the chest with just enough force to stop him solidly. After this initial contact, the blocker resets himself ready to take the rusher on again.

As the defender recovers and resumes his rush, the offensive lineman executes a parallel body block on him, to cut him down, so that the passer can see and throw.

COACHING TIPS: The blocker must jab-step and drop back in position *quickly*. In the initial lunge to stop the rusher, the blocker should not overextend himself forward, but rather he should block *up* through the rusher. This technique enables him to regather himself and to reset quickly. This initial lunge must be up through the middle of the defender while the blocker keeps his fists up under his chin and his elbows close down by his side.

After the first lunge and the following repositioning, the blocker cuts down the defender by throwing his inside shoulder hard through the outside leg of the defender and ending up in a high body block parallel to the line of scrimmage and directly across the path of the pass rusher.

Throwback Protection Drills: A difficult technique for an aggressive lineman to master is that of not overextending his weight forward while butting a pass rusher.

To teach this technique, we place a man on defense with a dummy in front of an offensive lineman in an offensive position. (See Figure 4–16.) The coach designates the onside, and on the snap the blocker jab-steps onside and drops back; then he butts the dummy brought hard by the defender. The defender tries to get around the blocker any way he can while the blocker butts, resets, slides for position, then butts again.

Figure 4–16. *Throwback protection drill.*

By letting young blockers butt and recover several times without using the body block, coaches can help them develop quickness, body balance, and feel for the block.

After the proper form, footwork, and balance have been developed for the butting and recovering techniques, the same drill can be used with the defender in aprons to put together the complete technique—the butt and the body block.

Blocking Stunts

For sound offensive football, it is necessary that an offensive line be able to handle certain basic stunts that might be used by the defense.

Various defensive stunts will minimize the effectiveness of certain offensive plays, but many plays can be run against most stunts, if certain precautions are taken to insure sound blocking.

The first prerequisite for the offense is that a full and thorough job of scouting be done on the opposition so that all defensive stunting combinations and situations in which they are used are known. Only plays that can be blocked against all known stunts should be used and included in the game plan.

Because of the basic differences in the alignment of odd and even type defenses and the possible stunting combinations, we break down stunts into two groups: (A) odd, or nine man front, (B) even, or eight man front.

(A) *Odd Defenses*

In the following diagrams (Figure 4–17) we will illustrate a basic odd defense and the stunting patterns most often used from this defensive alignment. We will then illustrate and discuss ways to block certain basic plays against these stunts. Keep in mind that certain stunts hurt certain plays, *but* the offensive line must have a plan for handling them so the plays will have a chance of success and blockers will not be at a complete loss as to what to do when they see these stunts.

Figure 4–17. *The most used stunts seen from the 5–2 defense.*

Figure 4–17 (a). *5–2 normal.*

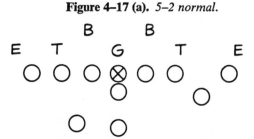

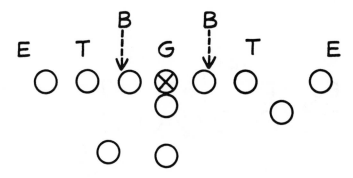

Figure 4–17 (b). *Linebacker blitz.*

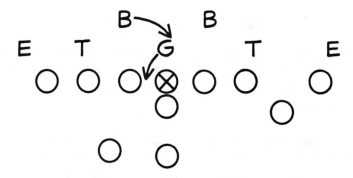

Figure 4–17 (c). *Linebacker-middle guard stunt.*

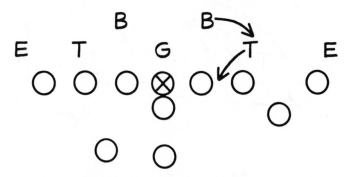

Figure 4–17 (d). *Linebacker-tackle stunt.*

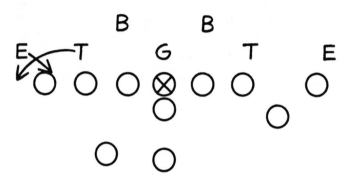

Figure 4–17 (e). *Tackle-end stunt.*

Now that we have established what stunts we will have to block, we will illustrate a means of blocking these basic plays against them: (1) Off tackle, (2) Isolation, (3) Trap, (4) Play action pass protection, and (5) Throwback pass.

Figure 4–18. *The off tackle play vs. stunts from the 5–2 defense. (For blocking rules see Chapter 1, page 21.)*

Figure 4–18 (1). *Off tackle play vs. straight 5–2 defense.*

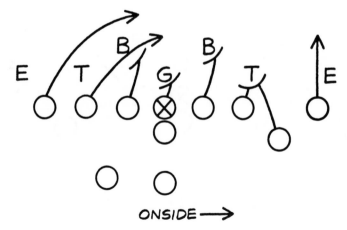

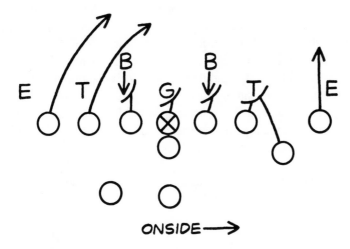

Figure 4–18 (2). *Off tackle play vs. linebacker blitz.*

The guards lunge out and drive block the blitzing linebacker normally. If the linebackers have lined up close to the line of scrimmage, the guards should anticipate a blitz.

Figure 4–18 (3). *Off tackle play vs. linebacker-middle guard stunt.*

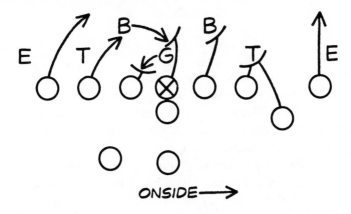

The normal blocking technique calls for the center to lunge out and drive block the left hip of the middle guard. The off guard should take a narrow split and step out with his right foot at the near hip of the middle guard. As both lunge out, the stunt will materialize. The center sees the middle guard slant away; hence, he should let him go and look for and pick up the offside linebacker who is taking the middle guard's responsibility. The offside guard, who has stepped toward the near hip of the middle guard, now blocks the middle guard, who is slanting at him.

If the middle guard is slanting toward the play, the center must be quick enough to block him. The offside guard, who has stepped out at the near hip of the middle guard, sees him go away; then he continues upfield to block the offside linebacker.

Figure 4–18 (4). *Off tackle play vs. linebacker-tackle stunt.*

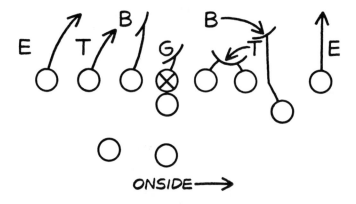

As the onside offensive tackle lunges out at the inside hip of the defensive tackle (see double team block, page 81), he will see him slant to the inside, and the offensive tackle should butt him on his outside hip and drive him to the inside. He should get help from the onside guard, who steps out with his right foot at an angle to cut off the linebacker, and who now faces the defensive tackle, slanting across his path.

The slotback lunges out at the outside hip of the defensive tackle, and as he sees the tackle's hip go away, he should look for and block the linebacker, who is stepping out to take the defensive tackle's responsibility.

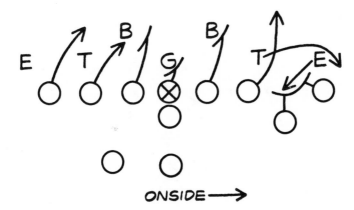

ONSIDE ——>

Figure 4–18 (5). *Off tackle play vs. tackle-end stunt.*

As the tackle, slotback, and end lunge out, the stunt will materialize. The end and slotback will pick up the end slanting into the slot area in front of them. The onside tackle should step out, see the stunt; then continue on downfield to block. The fullback now blocks out on the defensive tackle, who has looped out to take the defensive end's responsibility.

Figure 4–19. *The isolation play vs. stunts from the 5–2 defense. (For blocking rules see Chapter 1, page 18.)*

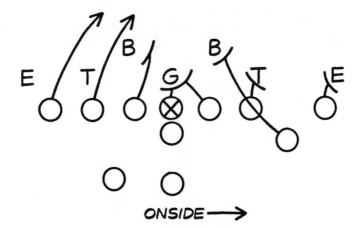

ONSIDE ——>

Figure 4–19 (1). *Isolation play vs. normal 5–2 defense.*

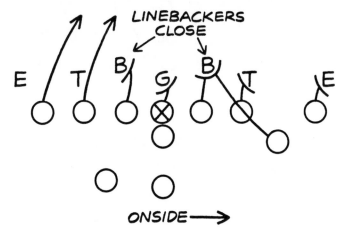

Figure 4–19 (2). *Isolation play vs. linebacker blitz.*

When the linebackers line up close to the line of scrimmage, the onside guard will not double team with the center. Instead, he will block the linebacker to keep him from penetrating the line of scrimmage.

COACHING POINT: We tell our offensive guard that if the linebacker's feet are as close to the line of scrimmage as the defensive lineman's feet, then he should block the linebacker. Also, the back leading into the hole should double team from the outside with the onside guard on the linebacker.

Figure 4–19 (3). *Isolation play vs. linebacker-middle guard stunt (middle guard slanting away).*

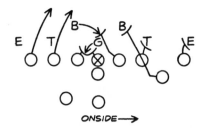

On the snap, the onside guard steps at the near hip of the defensive middle guard. The center steps out to butt the defensive middle guard, and the offside guard steps out at the near hip of the middle guard. As the stunt materializes, the center and the offside guard end up with a double team block on the defensive middle guard. The onside guard sees the near hip of the defensive guard go away; so he should look for and pick up with a left shoulder drive block the offside linebacker, who is stepping toward him to take the middle guard's responsibility.

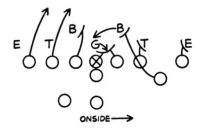

Figure 4–19 (4). *Isolation play vs. linebacker-middle guard stunt (middle guard slanting toward the play).*

The three middle offensive linemen step out the same as above. This time the center and onside guard double team the middle guard slanting between them while the offside guard sees the middle guard move away; then he moves on upfield at an angle to cut off the offside linebacker.

Figure 4–19 (5). *Isolation play vs. linebacker-tackle stunt.*

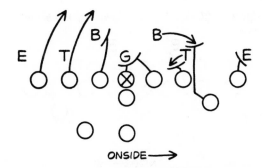

As the onside tackle lunges out at the near hip of the defensive tackle, he sees the tackle slant across his head toward the inside. He should butt the defensive tackle right in the middle of his body and take him to the inside, staying with him, and running him to the inside. The isolation now takes place between the defensive tackle and the defensive end.

The offside offensive tackle releases inside the offside defensive tackle in order to block downfield. If the stunt occurs on the offside, the offside offensive tackle should pick up the defensive tackle as the defensive tackle slants to the inside and across the face of the releasing tackle.

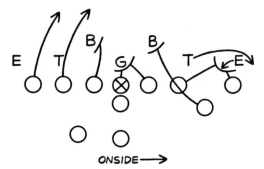

Figure 4–19 (6). *Isolation play vs. tackle-end stunt.*

The onside offensive end's responsibility on the isolation play is to turn out on the defensive end. He does this as the onside offensive tackle blocks out on the defensive tackle looping to the outside. This defensive stunt really opens the hole for the offense.

If the stunt occurs on the side away from the play, no adjustments are necessary. The offside offensive tackle releases normally to block downfield.

Figure 4–20. *The fullback trap vs. the 5–2 defense and stunts. (For blocking rules, see Chapter 1, page 14.)*

Figure 4–20 (1). *Fullback trap vs. a normal 5–2 defense.*

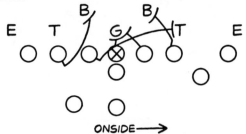

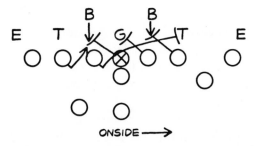

Figure 4–20 (2). *Fullback trap vs. the linebacker blitz.*

When the linebackers line up in a blitzing position, the center, guards, and tackles must be aware of this. The center immediately blocks the off linebacker without slamming the middle guard. The onside tackle does not influence the defensive tackle, but immediately blocks the defensive linebacker.

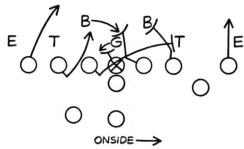

Figure 4–20 (3). *Fullback trap vs. linebacker-middle guard stunt.*

The center and the onside guard will handle this stunt in the same manner that they do the isolation play. (See Figure 4–19.)

Figure 4–20 (4). *Fullback trap vs. linebacker-tackle stunt.*

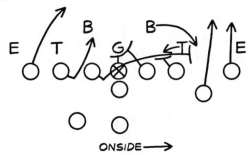

As the onside offensive tackle steps towards the near linebacker, the defensive tackle will slant across his path. The offensive tackle then should block the defensive tackle to the inside. The trapping guard now traps the defensive linebacker who is stepping out to take the defensive tackle's responsibility.

On the offside, the offside offensive tackle must anticipate this stunt, and he must be able to cut off the defensive tackle if he pinches to the inside.

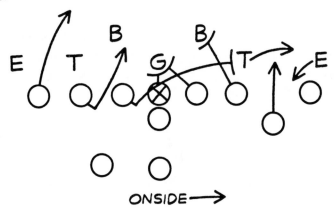

Figure 4–20 (5). *Fullback trap vs. tackle-end stunt.*

The offensive ends release inside the defensive ends. The rest of the blocking on this play is normal.

Figure 4–21. *Play action pass protection vs. the 5–2 defense and stunts. (For blocking rules, see Chapter 6, page 146.)*

Figure 4–21 (1). *Play action pass protection vs. normal 5–2 defense.*

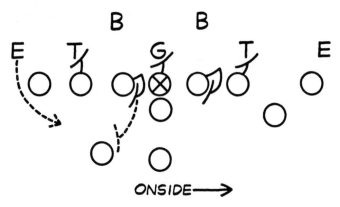

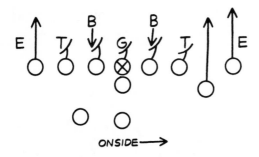

Figure 4–21 (2). *Play action pass protection vs. linebacker blitz.*

Against the stunt, the offensive guards block the blitzing linebackers aggressively after stepping forward and to the onside to protect the onside gaps.

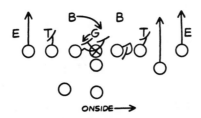

Figure 4–21 (3). *Play action pass protection vs. linebacker-middle guard stunt (middle guard slanting toward the play).*

In play action protection, we block "man,"—that is, we assign a certain defender to each offensive blocker. Against the 5–2 defenses, we assign the center to the middle guard and the offensive guards to the linebackers. Therefore, the center aggressively blocks the middle guard, and the guards check and block the linebackers who are rushing the passer.

Figure 4–21 (4). *Play action pass protection vs. linebacker-middle guard stunt (middle guard slanting toward the play).*

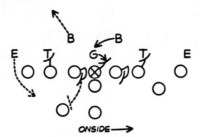

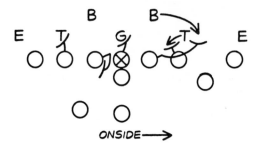

Figure 4–21 (5). *Play action pass protection vs. linebacker-tackle stunt.*

By blocking "man" we assign the tackle to the defensive tackle, while the offensive guard is responsible for stepping forward and to the onside, reading the stunt and stepping around the tackle to aggressively block the linebacker if he blitzes.

If the stunt occurs on the offside, the tackle is responsible for blocking the defensive tackle while the offside guard is responsible for stepping forward and to the onside, reading the stunt, then stepping back to aggressively block the linebacker if he blitzes.

Figure 4–21 (6). *Play action pass protection vs. tackle-end stunt.*

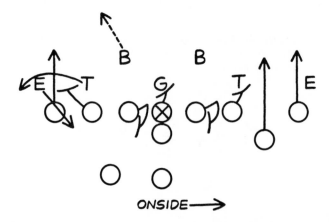

In our "man" scheme of blocking, the onside offensive tackle blocks the defensive tackle and follows him, as the defensive tackle loops to the outside while maintaining contact and driving him to the outside.

If the stunt occurs on the offside, the offside offensive tackle aggressively blocks the defensive tackle who is looping to the outside.

Figure 4–22. *Throwback pass protection vs. 5–2 defenses and stunts. (For blocking rules, see Chapter 6, page 169.)*

Figure 4–22 (1). *Throwback pass protection vs. normal 5–2 defense.*

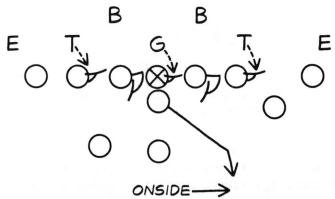

In our normal throwback protection, our linemen line up 6 inches off the ball and step laterally to the onside for position; then block any man coming into their area using a butt, and follow-up technique. (See page 87, this chapter.)

Figure 4–22 (2). *Throwback pass protection vs. linebacker blitz.*

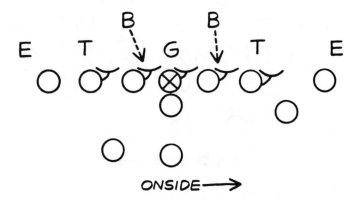

All linemen step onside and block in their respective areas. The guards block the blitzing linebackers using the normal throwback protection technique.

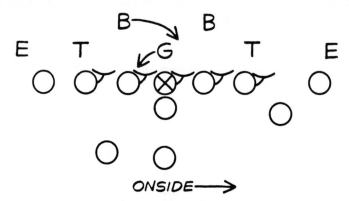

Figure 4–22 (3). *Throwback pass protection vs. linebacker-middle guard stunts.*

The center and guards step toward the onside and read the stunt (regardless of which way it develops), then each blocks the man coming into his area using the normal throwback protection technique.

Figure 4–22 (4). *Throwback pass protection vs. linebacker-tackle stunt.*

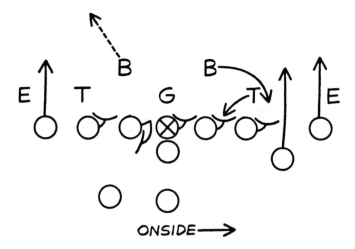

The onside offensive guard and tackle step toward the onside, read the stunt; then each blocks the men coming into his area.

If the stunt occurs on the offside, the offside guard and tackle handle the stunt in the same manner.

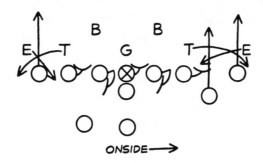

Figure 4–22 (5). *Throwback pass protection vs. tackle-end stunt.*

The onside offensive tackle steps to the onside and blocks the defensive end coming into his area.

If the stunt occurs on the offside, the tackle steps to the onside and blocks the end coming into his area.

(B) *Even Defenses*

In the following diagram (Figure 4–23) we will illustrate the basic even defense and the stunting patterns most often used from this defensive alignment. We will then illustrate and discuss ways to block certain basic plays against these stunts.

Figure 4–23. *The loose tackle six defense and its most used stunting combinations.*

Figure 4–23 (a). *Basic 6–2 defense.*

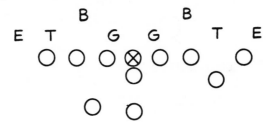

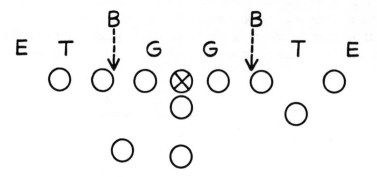

Figure 4–23 (b). *Linebacker blitz.*

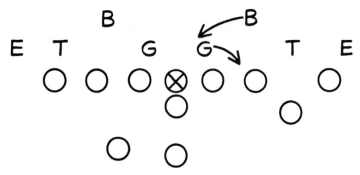

Figure 4–23 (c). *Linebacker-guard stunt.*

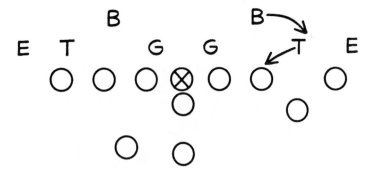

Figure 4–23 (d). *Linebacker-tackle stunt.*

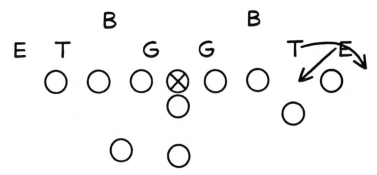

Figure 4–23 (e). *Tackle-end stunt.*

Now we shall illustrate a means of blocking these basic plays against the basic stunts illustrated: (1) off tackle power, (2) isolation, (3) trap, (4) play action pass protection, (5) throwback pass protection.

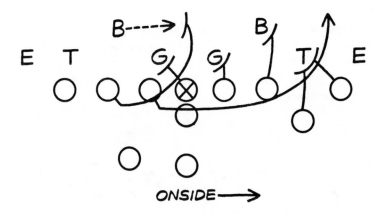

Figure 4–24. *The off tackle play vs. the 6–2 defense and stunts. (For blocking rules, see Chapter 1, page 21.)*

Figure 4–24 (1). *The off tackle play vs. 6–2 normal.*

We use normal 0, 1, 2, 3, 4 blocking rules on our off tackle power play with the onside guard and end using shoulder drive blocks, and the onside tackle using a running shoulder drive block.

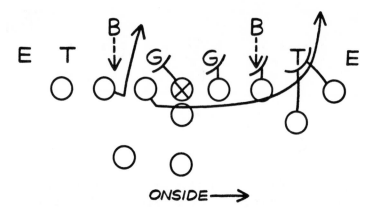

Figure 4–24 (2). *The off tackle play vs. linebacker blitz.*

The onside blocking is the same as against the normal 6–2 except that, in this case, the onside tackle uses a shoulder drive block against the linebacker blitzing over him.

The offside tackle releases inside the blitzing linebacker; thus, eliminating the linebacker's chances of figuring in on the play.

Figure 4–24 (3). *The off tackle play vs. linebacker-guard stunt.*

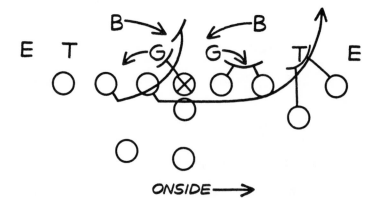

The onside defensive guard loops to the outside and becomes double teamed by the onside offensive guard, who is blocking him, and by the onside offensive tackle who steps out at the linebacker. But the onside offensive tackle is forced to help on the defensive guard looping across his face. This double team block cuts off the onside defensive linebacker, who should not figure in on the play.

On the offside, the offensive center blocks the guard who is looping to the outside, and the tackle pulls and blocks the offside defensive linebacker who is stepping to the inside.

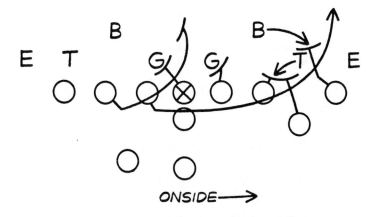

Figure 4–24 (4). *The off tackle play vs. linebacker-tackle stunt.*

The onside offensive tackle, end, and slotback handle this stunt. The defensive tackle, pinching to the inside, becomes double teamed by the slotback, who blocks him, and by the onside offensive tackle, who steps out at the linebacker, but the onside offensive tackle is forced to block the defensive tackle pinching across his face.The onside offensive end steps out at the near hip of the defensive tackle, and as that hip goes to the inside the end should look for and block the onside defensive linebacker, who is looping to the outside, by using a shoulder drive block.

On the offside, the offensive tackle releases inside the offside defensive linebacker normally. The offside defenders should not be able to figure in on the play.

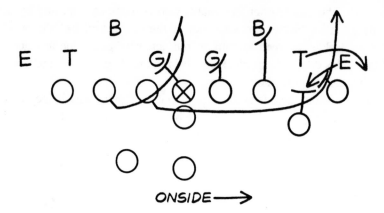

Figure 4–24 (5). *The off tackle play vs. tackle-end stunt.*

When the slotback and the onside offensive end step out at the defensive tackle, they will be forced to double team the defensive end pinching into the slot. The fullback will turn out on the defensive tackle, who has taken the defensive end's containment responsibility.

Figure 4–25. *Isolation play vs. the 6–2 defense and stunts. (For blocking rules, see Chapter 1, page 18.)*

Figure 4–25 (1). *Isolation play vs. 6–2 normal.*

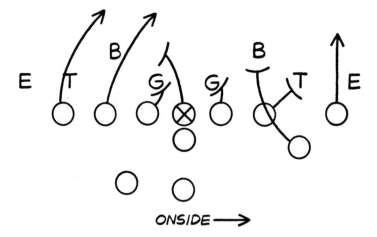

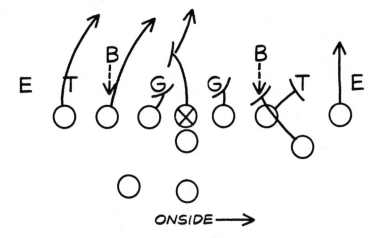

Figure 4–25 (2). *Isolation play vs. linebacker blitz.*

The blocking is the same as against a normal 6–2. The slotback must anticipate the blitz, and block the blitzing linebacker quickly before the linebacker can get penetration.

The offside offensive tackle must release inside the blitzing linebacker and block downfield. The center, who normally blocks the offside linebacker, sees that he has blitzed and also releases downfield to block.

Figure 4–25 (3). *Isolation play vs. linebacker-guard stunt.*

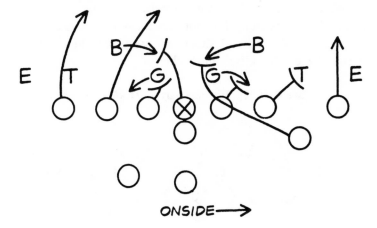

On the onside, the offensive guard turns out on the defensive guard, who is looping to the outside. Stepping to the inside, the slotback blocks the area at the point of attack for the linebacker. The isolation now occurs inside the defensive guard.

The offside guard turns out on the defensive guard, who is looping to the outside, and the center blocks the offside defensive linebacker as the linebacker steps to the inside.

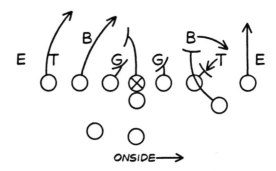

ONSIDE——>

Figure 4–25 (4). *Isolation play vs. linebacker-tackle stunt.*

On the onside, the offensive tackle blocks out on the defensive tackle who is pinching in through him. Because of the offensive tackle's angle, he should be able to make the block. If the linebacker has not run himself out of the play, the slotback leads up in the hole and blocks him. If the linebacker is gone, the slotback blocks downfield.

On the offside, the stunt does not create any problems since the offside offensive tackle and end should release downfield to block. The center should block the offside linebacker.

Figure 4–25 (5). *Isolation play vs. tackle-end stunt.*

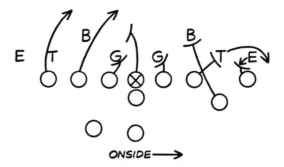

ONSIDE——>

On the onside, the offensive end blocks out on the defensive end normally, and the offensive tackle blocks out on the defensive tackle.

On the offside, no special adjustments are necessary since the offside offensive end and tackle release to block downfield.

Figure 4–26. *The fullback trap vs. the 6–2 defense and stunts. (For blocking rules, see Chapter 1, page 14.)*

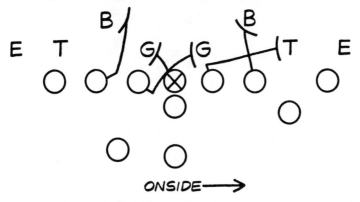

Figure 4–26 (1). *The fullback trap vs. normal 6–2 defense.*

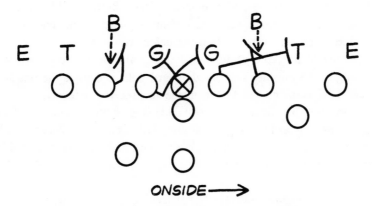

Figure 4–26 (2). *The fullback trap vs. linebacker blitz.*

On the onside, the offensive tackle's normal assignment is the linebacker; so, he blocks him with a shoulder drive block, with the main point being not to let the linebacker surprise him and beat him to the inside. The onside guard influences the defensive guard and then turns out on the defensive tackle.

On the offside, the guard pulls and traps. The offside tackle steps with the guard and turns upfield and blocks the offside defensive linebacker. (This is normal technique vs. 6–2 defense against the blitz.) Since the tackle steps to pull, he will see the blitz develop and will cut off the linebacker immediately, rather than continue his pull technique.

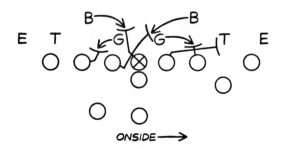

Figure 4–26 (3). *The fullback trap vs. linebacker-guard stunt.*

On the snap of the ball, the stunt should develop. On the onside, as the offensive guard and tackle step out, the defensive guard loops in front of the offensive tackle and becomes blocked by the tackle. The onside offensive guard steps toward the defensive guard to influence him, sees him loop, and then turns out on the defensive tackle.

On the offside, the center steps out at the defensive guard, who is looping to the outside. The offside guard pulls and traps the onside linebacker, who has moved to the inside to take the defensive guard's responsibility. The offside offensive tackle steps with the guard and blocks the defensive guard looping out at him. The center now blocks the offside defensive linebacker who is moving to the inside to take the offside defensive guard's responsibility.

Figure 4–26 (4). *The fullback trap vs. linebacker-tackle stunt.*

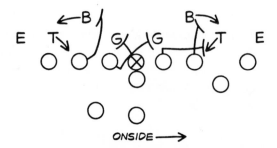

The onside offensive guard influences the defensive guard; then he turns out and blocks the pinching defensive tackle. The onside offensive guard's main objective is to keep the stunting tackle from surprising him. The onside offensive tackle blocks the defensive linebacker who is looping to the outside.

On the offside, the blocking is normal with the center blocking the offside defensive guard; the offside offensive guard pulling and trapping; and the offside offensive tackle stepping onside and turning up to block the offside defensive linebacker.

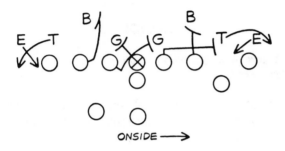

Figure 4–26 (5). *The fullback trap vs. tackle-end stunt.*

On the onside, blocking is normal except that the offensive guard influences and then blocks out on the pinching defensive end.

On the offside, all blocking is the same as for the normal 6–2.

Figure 4–27. *Play action pass protection vs. the 6–2 defense and stunts. (For blocking rules, see Chapter 6, page 146.)*

Figure 4–27 (1). *Play action pass protection vs. 6–2 normal.*

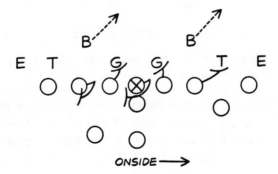

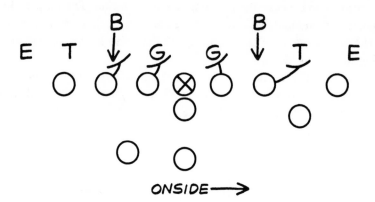

Figure 4–27 (2). *Play action pass protection vs. linebacker-blitz.*

To protect against a four-man rush on the onside, an extra back must be used, in order to assure sound protection. (See solid protection rules, Chapter 6, page 175.)

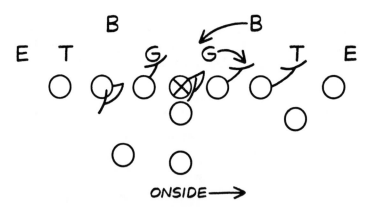

Figure 4–27 (3). *Play action pass protection vs. linebacker-guard stunt.*

On the onside, the offensive guard drives the defensive guard who is looping to the outside. The linebacker should not be able to loop to the inside and catch a fast-moving, play action pass wide to the onside. If the pass is a slow developing one, and the linebacker can catch it, then special protection must be used to handle the four-man rush on the onside. (See solid protection, Chapter 6, page 175.)

The offside blocking is normal. The center steps onside and if the onside linebacker blitzes, he blocks him. If the onside linebacker does not blitz, the center then checks the offside linebacker. If the linebacker blitzes, then the center blocks him. If the center checks both linebackers and they are not blitzing, he next checks the offside rushers and blocks the first one to threaten the play.

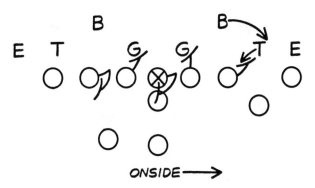

Figure 4–27 (4). *Play action pass protection vs. linebacker-tackle stunt.*

On the onside, the offensive tackle reaches and drives the pinching tackle. If the linebacker loops and blitzes, then special protection must be used to protect against the four-man rush on the onside. (See solid protection rules, Chapter 6, page 175.)

On the offside, the offensive tackle steps toward the linebacker and then turns out when the linebacker loops to the outside. As the tackle turns out, he should block the defensive tackle, who is pinching in on him.

Figure 4–27 (5). *Play action pass protection vs. tackle-end stunt.*

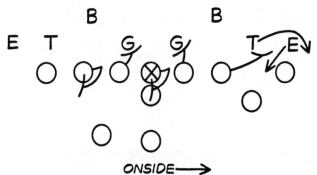

On the onside, the offensive tackle reaches the looping tackle and blocks him. The back blocks the defensive end normally.

On the offside, the offensive tackle checks the linebacker and then turns out to take the first rusher threatening the play. In this case, it is the defensive end who is pinching.

Figure 4–28. *Throwback pass protection vs. the 6–2 defense and stunts. (For blocking rules, see Chapter 6, page 146.)*

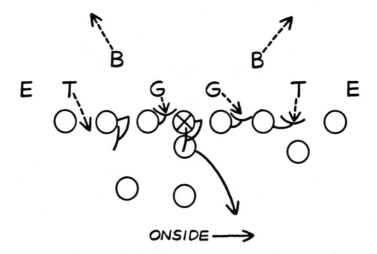

Figure 4–28 (1). *Throwback pass protection vs. 6–2 normal.*

Figure 4–28 (2). *Throwback pass protection vs. linebacker blitz.*

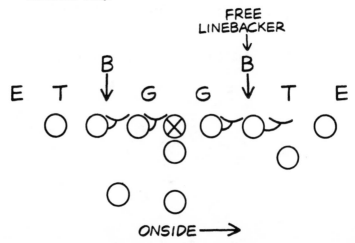

Special protection must be used to handle a four-man rush on the onside. (See solid protection, Chapter 6, page 175.)

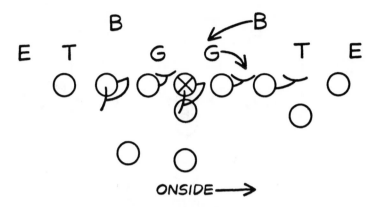

ONSIDE⟶

Figure 4–28 (3). *Throwback pass protection vs. linebacker-guard stunt.*

The onside offensive guard position steps and takes the looping guard when he rushes. If the looping linebacker blitzes, special protection must be used to handle the four-man rush on the onside. (See solid protection, Chapter 6, page 175.)

Figure 4–28 (4). *Throwback pass protection vs. linebacker-tackle stunt.*

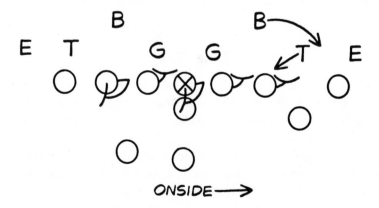

ONSIDE⟶

The onside offensive tackle blocks the pinching tackle when he rushes. If the looping linebacker blitzes, special protection must be used to protect against the four-man rush on the onside. (See solid protection, Chapter 6, page 175.)

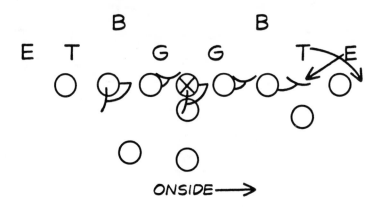

Figure 4–28 (5). *Throwback pass protection vs. tackle-end stunt.*

The onside offensive tackle takes a position step and blocks the pinching end who is coming into the defensive tackle's normal rushing lane.

As a summary, it can be stated that the basic blocking schemes illustrated in the preceding pages against the various defenses and stunting combinations can be adapted for use on many types of plays with all types of backfield action.

Line Calls

Certain plays can be better blocked by exchanging the blocking assignments of various offensive blockers. Also, certain defenses necessitate the modification of blocking assignments in order to get stronger "first wave" blocking.

The use of such calls is normal procedure when we face a team that may be using two or three different defenses during a game, or when we face a team that jumps from one defense to another after we have assumed our offensive alignment. We also make line calls when our offensive linemen detect that the defense is cheating its alignment in

order to execute a stunt. Then a change of assignments is needed in order
to handle the stunt.

We use line calls (verbal signals made after we have lined up and
become set) to exchange assignments, or to get stronger blocking at the
point of attack, or to remind other linemen that certain conditions exist
relevant to the play that is to be run. These calls take precedence over
normal rules on any play that they are used.

These are the line calls that we use: (1) Double, (2) Cross, (3)
Swing, (4) Reach, and (5) Gap.

(1) "Double"—This is a call used by the guard to let the tackle know
that his (the guard's) man is outside and that he will need help in order
to block him. (See Figure 4–29.)

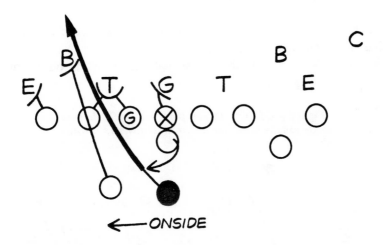

Figure 4–29. *Isolation vs. eagle defense. (The
guard makes the "Double" call.)*

On this play the tackle normally blocks out until he hears the
"Double" call.

(2) "Cross"—This signal is used to insure against certain stunts and
is simply an exchange of blocking assignments between two offensive
blockers with the inside man going first. (See Figure 4–30.)

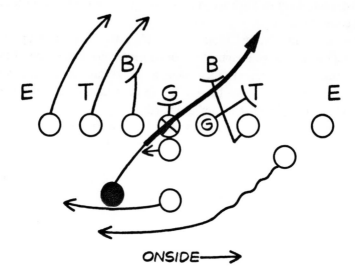

Figure 4–30. *Veer play vs. 5–2 defense. (The tackle makes the "Cross" call.)*

On this play, the onside guard usually blocks the linebacker and the onside tackle, the defensive tackle.

(3) "Swing"—This is like the "Cross" call except that the outside man goes first. (See Figure 4–31.)

Figure 4–31. *Off tackle play vs. stack defense. Tackle usually takes linebacker until he hears "Swing" call.*

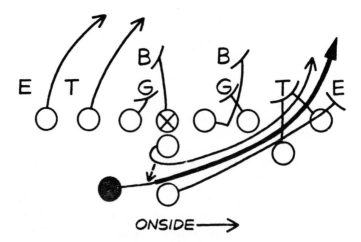

(4) "Reach"—This signal is used in pass protection blocking when the center is uncovered. It requires the center and one side of the offensive line to block the first man outside them on the onside. This is one means of protecting against a four-man blitz on the onside, against even defenses. (See Figure 4–32.)

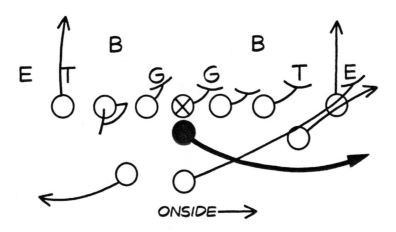

Figure 4–32. *Play action pass vs. loose tackle six defense.*

(5) "Gap"—A signal used to alert the offense that the defense is in a gap type defense, and that everyone who has a man in his inside gap should block to the inside. (See Figure 4–33.)

Figure 4–33. *Off tackle vs. gap eight.*

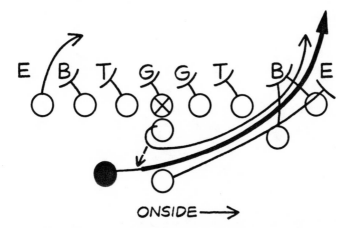

Our offensive ends have to be a combination of interior linemen and offensive backs. They are called on for four major duties. These duties are the following:

A. Blocking
   1. Line of scrimmage
   2. Downfield
B. Punt coverage
   1. Protection
   2. Coverage
C. Pass receiver
   1. Release from line of scrimmage
   2. Routes
   3. Catching the ball
D. Ballcarrier

5

In order to best accomplish the above responsibilities, we have utilized our personnel as either "tight ends" or "split ends," although we do not always have a split end formation. By doing this,

Coaching the
Offensive Ends

we have been able to specialize our personnel and of course this means that we can use our strongest blockers as tight ends while using our more agile pass receivers and downfield blockers as split ends. We feel, as most coaches do today, that this is one way to help solve the problem of too little practice time as well as an opportunity to utilize the best abilities of our individual players.

Blocking in Ball-Control Offense

Stance: The stance used by the offensive end, both tight and split, is the same one that is used by the offensive linemen. (The stance is described in Chapter 4, page 66.)

Types of Blocks

1. The Drive Block: This block is the one most often used by the offensive end. This drive block is used often in the one-on-one situations where the end is required to block a defender by himself. For example, the ends block on the defensive tackle when running against the loose tackle 6–2 defense. Often the end is mismatched with the tackle in overall size and strength; therefore, he must make up for the difference in size and strength with technique. This means that the end must have the best stance, the best start, and that he must be quicker than the tackle.

The drive block technique used by the offensive end is the same one that is used by the interior offensive linemen. (See Chapter 4, page 71 for a description of the drive block and the drive blocking drills.)

2. The Reverse Shoulder Block: This technique is used by the offensive end in blocking a defensive tackle in a loose tackle six defense on the split T option play. The offensive end should start the block exactly like the drive block, and when the defender reacts to the inside, as the ball is faked to the halfback, he should use the reverse shoulder block to drive him to the inside.

The reverse shoulder drive block technique used by the offensive end is the same one that is used by the interior offensive linemen. (See Chapter 4 page 77 for a description of the reverse shoulder block and the reverse shoulder blocking drills.)

3. Double Team: The double team block consists of the post and drive blocks. In a tight slot, the end's block is normally the drive block on the double team. Therefore, we will discuss the total block and describe it from the tight slot. The post block will be performed by the slotback and the drive block will be executed by the end.

The slotback should execute drive block techniques in order to complete the post block. One important coaching point is that he should aim at the inside hip of the defender rather than at his belt buckle. This point is actually only a couple of inches away from the belt buckle, but it serves as a reminder to our slotback that he is responsible first for preventing any penetration. If the defender should slant inside, aiming at the defender's inside hip will help the slotback accomplish his block. The slotback's technique now becomes the reverse shoulder block previously described. If the defender uses a normal charge, the slotback's drive block should be executed with his first responsibility being to prevent penetration and his second responsibility to prevent the double team block from being split. The slotback's first job is accomplished by his firing out on the count and by his stepping with the inside foot and executing the drive block technique. The slotback's second responsibility —preventing the double team from being split—is accomplished by his working his buttocks to the outside to the drive block by the end.

On the double team, the end should execute a drive block by lead stepping with his inside foot at the belt buckle of the defender. The end's first responsibility is not to allow the double team block to be split. The end's second responsibility is to lock his head, neck, and shoulders tight against the defender and to prevent him from rolling out of the double team.

Jointly then, the double team block should prevent penetration and it should not allow the defender to roll out to pursue. In order to better accomplish the above, the blockers should drive the defender off the line of scrimmage and backward in as straight a line as possible. The blockers are not trying to turn the defender, rather they are attempting to drive him straight off the line of scrimmage in order to help cut off pursuit. As a coaching point we ask the double team blockers to continue their block until the whistle ending the play is blown.

4. Downfield Blocking: Downfield blocking is a matter of pride and effort. It is a difficult assignment but one that can be accomplished by any football player who "wants to play." The number one consideration is for the blocker to sprint downfield and commit on every single play. To do this, the blocker must know whom he is supposed to block. The blocker is assigned to a specific defensive man on each play and he should go to this man via the most direct route.

A list of the basic steps for the downfield block is the following: (1) know the assignment, (2) know the stance, (3) use a quick release from the line of scrimmage, (4) take the most direct route to the defender, and (5) commit the defender.

The downfield block will vary depending on how the defender is approached. If the defender retreats, the end should attempt to run over him and he should not commit until he is in a position close enough to jab the defender with his forehead. If the end overtakes the defender, he should use a cross-body block on him. The blocker should roll over two or three times on the ground in order to maintain contact with the defender and to try to tie up the defender's feet.

Should the end have a blind side approach to the defender, he will attempt to run straight through him, aiming his own forehead at the defender's chin. In this case, the end should not leave the ground. This insures against clipping.

A coaching point we use is that we insist the end sprint to the point of attack and *never* look back at the ball. He should look at the defender and attack him.

5. The Peelback Block: This block is used on all pass plays by all eligible receivers not receiving the ball after the ball is thrown and completed. The forehead is aimed at the defender's chin and the blocker does not leave his feet but runs through the defender. The nearest man to the receiver attacks the defender closest to the receiver and all others "peel" to the ball. The result is usually a blind side block which can be a vicious one. This is a matter of discipline and pride and our boys have accepted the challenge to be in on every pass—if not as receiver, then as a "peelback blocker."

Offensive End Blocking Drills

We have described the four basic blocking techniques that are used by the offensive ends. Our most experienced ends, as well as the inexperienced ones, are drilled every day in these basic blocking techniques.

  (a) *The crowther sled drills.*
       (1) The offensive ends use the Hit! Hit! Hit! drill that is used by the offensive linemen. (For a description of the Hit! Hit! Hit! drill see Chapter 4, page 72.)

(2) The offensive ends use the hit and drive sled drill that is used by the offensive linemen. (For a description of the hit and drive drill see Chapter 4, page 73.)

(3) The offensive ends use the hit and drive drill and utilize a free sled (no one on the sled) in order to teach the ends to maintain contact with a soft-playing defender. The blocker must use a wide base, and he must use short, quick steps in order to maintain contact.

(b) *The board drills.*

(1) The board blocking drills that are used by the offensive ends are the same board drills that are used by the offensive linemen. (For a description of the board blocking drills see Chapter 4, pages 73–74.)

Punt Coverage

From a seven-man front spread punt formation, the ends are the contain men and must sprint to maintain width and field position on the punt receiver. His job is as follows: (1) to protect the kicker, (2) cover the punt, and (3) contain the punt returner by turning him inside or making the tackle.

The techniques of slamming and releasing primarily determine the speed of coverage. Individual speed is the key factor, but because protection is the end's first responsibility, the technique of slamming is more important.

The offensive end must be able to tackle. This may sound like an unusual statement, but with platoon football the only tackling that the offensive end is instructed to do is on punts, field goal coverage, and pass interceptions. Therefore, we must work extra hard on this because his tackle in any of these situations is a "must tackle." We are not interested in his making a punishing tackle but rather a safe, high tackle.

To accomplish the above, we use the following rules and drills for protection, coverage, and tackling.

(a) **Protection:** Our end's rule is to take a 3-foot split unless there is an overload between the end and the tackle. If there is an overload (two or more defenders between the end and tackle), the end will cut his split to 2 feet in width and he will keep his inside foot in place as he drop-steps with this outside foot at approximately a 45 degree angle. He remains in a low hitting position and he should slam to the outside using a forearm lift while maintaining his inside foot in place. The slam must stop the defender's charge. If his initial charge is stopped, the time involved will give the kicker the necessary time to get the punt off. Should there be no inside overload, the end will butt and run through the first defender to the outside and he will then get in the proper route for coverage.

(b) Tackling: Tackling form is stressed in drills but we usually work on open field tackling at full speed. We do form head-on and across-the-bow tackling, with the end tackling a defender lined up about 4 or 5 yards away. The open field tackling drill that has been used with success is the following: (See Figure 5–1.) We line up an end and a punt returner about 15 yards apart. The end should sprint at the punt receiver. After the end has run 5 yards, the punt returner starts running at him, and after running 5 yards, returner will break to one side or the other and try to evade the end. The end comes under control, assumes a good hitting position, and then stalks the punt returner and tackles him using an across-the-bow tackle. The end must use good tackling form and he must stop the runner by tackling "safe."

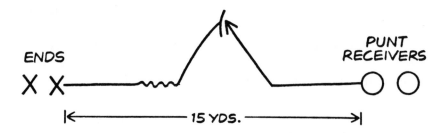

Figure 5–1. *The open field tackling drill.*

The End as a Pass Receiver

(1) The Release from the Line of Scrimmage: You will note that we have listed pass receiving as an important requirement for our offensive ends. However, when a pass is thrown, the number one requirement for the end is to catch the football.

There are actually three phases in catching the football: (1) getting off the line of scrimmage—the release, (2) running the proper pass route —getting open, (3) receiving the ball.

To get off the line of scrimmage, the end must assume the proper stance and get off on the count. As mentioned earlier, this is a basic step in offensive football. There are three techniques used by our ends to get off the line of scrimmage other than utilizing wide splits:

(a) Fake—The fake is usually a head and shoulder fake to one side, and then releasing quickly with a short, quick step in the opposite direction. The end must come off the line of scrimmage as low as possible after the fake. The end's speed and quickness are extremely important.

(b) Scramble—The end may release from the line of scrimmage by scrambling out on all fours. Usually he will dip to one side of the defender and by staying low will release under the hands or forearms of the defender. As soon as he clears the line of scrimmage, the end should come up as quickly as possible and immediately get on the called pass route.

(c) Butt—The third method of clearing the line of scrimmage is having the end butt the defender in exactly the way he would to start the one-on-one drive block, and then release as quickly as possible on his assigned pass route.

2. The End's Hands: The basic requirement needed in actually catching the football is good "hands." An athlete must have some natural ability in this area but anyone can improve his catching with work. A pass receiver must know that he can catch the football and he must take great pride in catching the football.

One of the cardinal rules in pass catching is for the end to run in a normal way and keep his hands in a normal running position until the last possible second. Then he reaches and takes the ball out of the air. As a basic rule, the thumbs should be apart to catch a ball below the waist and the thumbs together to catch a ball above the waist. As the ball is caught with both hands, the end should tuck the ball in and put it away. Normally the end should drop his lead shoulder as he turns upfield and run for the goal line.

The receiver must "know" that he can catch any ball and he must have pride in his ability to do so.

3. The Receiving Drills: Every practice is started with an all pass drill where a quarterback will have four or five receivers and two footballs. (See Figure 5–2.) The receiver should catch the ball on the fourth or fifth step while utilizing these principles: (1) good running form, (2) keeping the hands in a normal running position until the last possible second, (3) locking the ball in as the end puts it away, and (4) dropping the lead shoulder in order to go for the goal line.

The quarterback, by using two footballs, can throw and complete many passes in this drill. He should change sides in order for the ends to receive balls from the right and left sides.

Finally, in the drill, the quarterback should throw several long passes. The receiver should run under the ball while utilizing the ball-catching principles listed above.

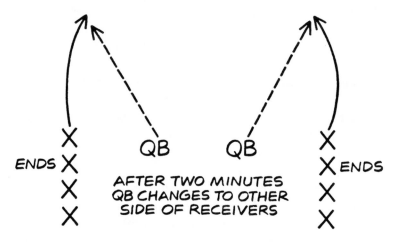

Figure 5-2. *The all pass drill.*

(a) The sideline passing drill—The end should execute a short flat route, catch the ball, and then fight to stay in bounds with several defenders attempting to knock him out-of-bounds. (See Figure 5–3.)

Figure 5-3. *The sideline passing drill.*

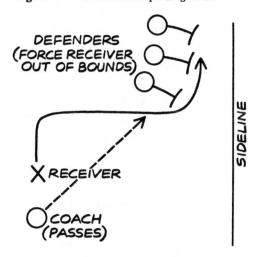

(b) **The in-bounds drill**—The same setup as diagrammed above is used except that the goal of this drill is to catch the ball in bounds. The receiver must have complete control of his body and know his exact position on the field in order to have possession before he steps out-of-bounds.

(c) **The concentration drill**—The end receives a short pass. He is then hit by two men holding dummies. The pass receiver must catch the ball, put it away, and become a tough runner. The goal of this drill is to develop concentration on catching the football and aggressiveness as a ballcarrier. (See Figure 5–4.)

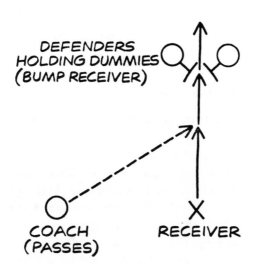

Figure 5–4. *The concentration drill.*

(d) **Bad pass drill**—This drill is to be used in connection with teaching all pass routes. A net is stretched between the goalposts on the practice field and the ball is thrown hard, soft, right, left, high, or low to the receiver who is running basic pass routes. The net will serve to stop the ball if the receiver misses the pass, thus saving time in retrieving the ball. (See Figure 5–5.) It is surprising how well an end can catch when he "believes he can catch anything that is thrown."

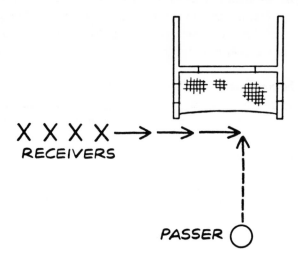

Figure 5–5. *The bad pass drill.*

Pass Routes

The end's release from the line of scrimmage and his having good hands are basic requirements, but his ability to properly execute the pass route is the most important factor in defeating the various defensive coverages. Whether the coverage is zone or man-to-man, perfect execution of the pass route is the key to getting open. In this phase of football, the only substitute for speed and quickness is finesse in execution of the route. When you have all three—speed, quickness, and route execution—you have the makings of an outstanding offensive pass receiver.

In the following material, nine of our basic pass routes will be diagrammed and briefly discussed. All of our receivers, ends, and backs, are expected to be able to execute these routes.

(a) The hook route—The straight hook is the route used to beat the linebacker, and is best utilized from our pull-up and throw-back action passes. The end should sprint off of the line of scrimmage at an angle that would carry him through the inside hip of a three-deep defensive halfback. He should sprint as far as his speed will enable him to go before the quarterback is ready to throw. Then, he will execute a basketball-type pivot, planting his outside foot and pivoting on his inside foot, and set up in a parallel stance with his feet no more than shoulder width apart. He should have his hands in a ready position in order to receive the ball. On the pivot, he should immediately read the linebacker. If the end is open he should catch the ball at this spot. If the linebacker has read the play and is sprinting to the hook zone, the end should slide to the inside in order to receive the pass. The end should *never* wait for the football but should go back to meet the ball on this route.

The end should drop his inside shoulder and turn up the field in order to attack the defender after receiving the pass. (See Figure 5–6.)

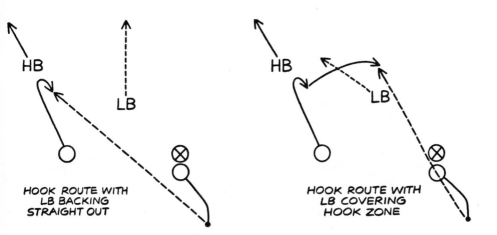

Figure 5–6. *The hook route.*

(b) The circle hook route—This route is usually executed by the split end and is designed to beat the linebacker. The end should sprint off the line of scrimmage and go toward the outside hip of the wide defender. The depth of the end's pattern is determined by his speed and the time it takes the quarterback to get set in order to throw.

As the end approaches the spot at which he will cut, he fakes with his head to the inside and breaks deep outside for a couple of steps; then he turns sharply to the inside. When the end makes his turn, he must read the linebacker. If the end is open, he should receive the ball immediately. If the linebacker is coming to the flat, the end should continue to the inside until he is open and then receive the pass. He should be careful not to circle too far inside because the safety man could cover him. If the ball is not thrown on the cut he must go to meet the ball.

Since the circle hook pattern is run from a split position, the end should be in a better position to become an open field runner. (See Figure 5–7.)

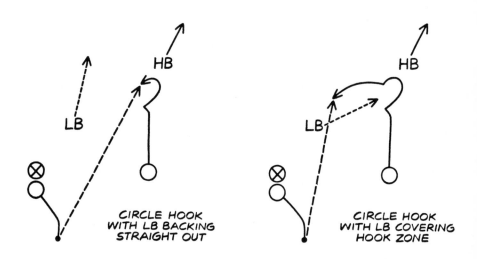

Figure 5–7. *The circle hook route.*

CIRCLE HOOK
WITH LB BACKING
STRAIGHT OUT

CIRCLE HOOK
WITH LB COVERING
HOOK ZONE

(c) The "out" route—The out pattern is designed to beat the wide defender with a timed cut out to the sideline. The end should drive off the line of scrimmage toward the outside hip of the defender. If the defender lines up outside of him, the end must still drive at the defender's outside hip in order to take this outside position away from the defender. Then, after utilizing a head and shoulder fake to the inside, the end should cut to the outside. The end should make the angle of his cut such that he is running slightly toward the line of scrimmage. By coming back toward the line of scrimmage, the offensive end widens the area between himself and the defender.

Depending on the situation, the receiver should now fight to stay in bounds for yardage or he can go out-of-bounds to stop the clock.

When a one-on-one situation has been created, it is next to impossible to stop the out cut if the execution of the route and the time of the pass are properly coordinated.

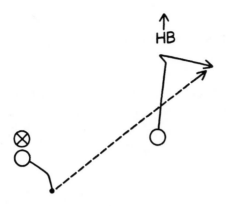

Figure 5-8. *The "out" pass route.*

(d) The bend-in route—The bend-in route is used to be able to throw in the seam between the safety man and the sideback in a three-deep zone. The end should release at the outside hip of the sideback, and at the proper time cut straight up the field. He must be careful not to go too far inside where the safety man can pick him up. The pass must be thrown on time because a late throw can be intercepted by the safety. We usually use this as a throwback type pass pattern where the size of the open area is likely to be increased when the safety starts toward the flow.

Figure 5-9. *The bend-in pass route.*

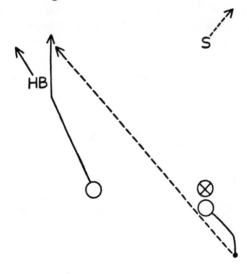

(e) The hitch route—This is a quick pass route to a wide receiver, and is thrown as soon as the quarterback can get ready to throw. The pass should be used after a one-on-one coverage situation is established. The receiver should start with his ouside foot first, take five steps, and hook as described under the hook route. The ball must be delivered immediately to the receiver. After catching the ball, the receiver should be in an open field running situation against one defender.

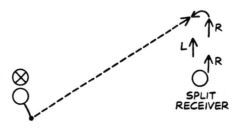

Figure 5–10. *The hitch route.*

(f) The flat route—The flat route is the primary route on the sprint out pass and is used to beat the zone coverage of the flat. The receiver on the flat route is working for width more than depth and will be sprinting to beat a linebacker, or to get width to stretch the defensive coverage. On the flat route, 5 to 7 yards should be the maximum depth. The receiver must work to turn his numbers to the quarterback. The receiver should look the ball in, drop his inside shoulder, and turn up the field running.

Figure 5–11. *The flat route.*

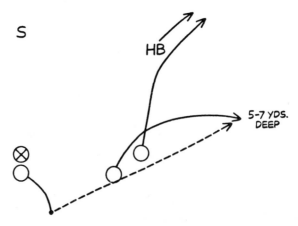

(g) The flag route—The flag route is the deep outside route used in our sprint out pass. The end should release through the sideback area, and if the sideback takes him, the end will continue to run for the flag. This angle will vary depending on where the ball is located on the snap. Should the defensive sideback "level" to the flat, the end should break away from the safety man.

This route is also used on many of our play passes and misdirection passes in order to clear the area for a crossing receiver. If the end can beat a defender deep on the flag route, he can make a touchdown.

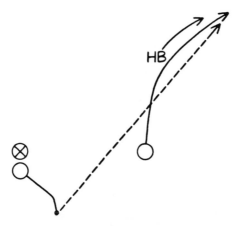

Figure 5–12. *The flag route.*

(h) The delay route—It is used primarily as a throwback type pass with the end setting up as if to pass block. (See Chapter 6, Figures 6–26 and 6–27 for illustration and description of the delay route.)

(i) The turkey route—The turkey route is a variation of the out cut, and it is illustrated and described in conjunction with the sprint out passing game. (See Chapter 6, Figure 6–20.)

Ballcarriers

It is important for a pass receiver to understand that he must first catch the football. But once the ball is secured we feel that he must become an aggressive runner.

The sideline drill and the concentration drills described above help us become pass receivers first and then runners. The details of our running techniques are covered in the chapter on backfield play.

$\mathbf{T}$he three basic elements of any passing attack are these:

1. The pass protection
2. The skill of the passer
3. The receivers.

If a team had to choose only one way to pass, and had to decide between the drop-back pass, the sprint out pass, and the play action pass, it should choose the latter. The play action passer, by its run faking action, minimizes the pass rush and thereby aids in the protection. It aids the pass because with good faking and/or misdirection action it requires less pinpoint passing, as the pass receiver is more likely to be open with the defenders more involved in play recognition. Finally, it helps the receiver because the play action fake will help hold the defenders—particularly the linebackers—since the linebackers must play the run first and then react in the pass coverage. Therefore, the receiver should not be as tightly covered as he might ordinarily be.

6

Honor the Run or Throw

Also in play action passes, the receiver is not called on to run highly timed pass cuts or routes, but instead is asked to run through a particular lane or zone to take advantage of a cleared or flooded area.

The disadvantages of the play action pass are these:

1. It is not a good choice on third down and long yardage or definite passing situations because the play action will not affect the coverage if the defense is expecting the pass.

2. If the defense is forcing or stunting, it creates a two-on-one situation for the offense to block; and in addition, since the quarterback must usually turn his back to the defense in order to fake, he will not be in a position to see the rush or be ready for it.

3. When facing the gap charge with eight defenders rushing, the quarterback is forced to abandon the fake completely and get rid of the ball quickly. Therefore, the faking action of the play is lost.

The basic advantages of play action passes are these:

1. The play action pass complements a strong running game by keeping the defense off balance and, by the design of the play, can create an option to run or pass.

2. It utilizes bootleg and misdirection plays which give the offense a much needed "change of pace."

3. By using play action passes on the nonpassing downs and in special situations such as short yardage, or after a changeover caused by a fumble or pass interception, or after a penalty, it gives the offense an opportunity to make the "big play."

4. By using the play action pass on the nonpassing down, the offense can avoid the third and long situation because the "bread and butter" ground plays should not be defensed as aggressively.

5. Play action passes provide a passing game for the quarterback who is not an exceptional passer.

6. Play action passes fit into the ground game philosophy because all play action passes should have the run as the first option.

As stated, the basic elements of any passing attack are pass protection, the passer, and the receivers.

The play action pass helps in the area of pass protection. By its nature the play action pass tends to neutralize the heavy rush, and eliminates the holding up of the receivers. Also it makes it more difficult for the defensive secondary, since the normal pass rush and normal harassment of pass receivers are great aids to pass coverage. This is assuming that the play action pass is called on a nonpassing down and that the defense is playing the run first. If the faking accomplishes this, it will become possible for the passer to get on the corner quickly with the option either to run or pass. On this type play, the good running quarterback is being used to do what he does best—carry the football.

In this type of play pass where the first option is to run, the passer should throw only if the receiver is wide open. This philosophy helps the average passer because he has only one decision to make regarding the pass; and that is—throw *only* if the receiver is wide open. If the play execution is good, the run fake should hold the linebackers and the problem of reading the coverage is held to a minimum. Reading the coverage is still of the utmost importance to the success of any type of pass.

On most play action passes the primary receiver is normally running a hidden, crossing, or delayed route, and this route gives him a chance to break into an open area and receive the ball while running in the open. In addition to this, a teammate has usually cleared the zone or area where the primary receiver will catch the ball and is in an excellent position to "peelback" block. Therefore, on play action passes, the receiver is running a basic pass route into an open area created by the rotation of the defense, the fake or a run, and other receivers clearing the zone. This gives the receiver an opportunity to catch the ball while running in a cleared area, thus minimizing the execution of the pass cut as he would normally be covered by a tight defender. It also affords the pass receiver an opportunity to utilize the "peelback" block of a teammate who has cleared the zone.

It is important to use a play action pass that looks like the basic "bread and butter" running plays in the offense. In other words, the best running plays in the offense should be complemented by a play action pass.

Four of our most successful play action passes along with blocking rules and coaching points will be illustrated in the following material.

The Fullback Trap Pass

The running play that this pass complements is discussed and diagrammed in Chapter 1. (See Chapter 1, Figure 1–21.)

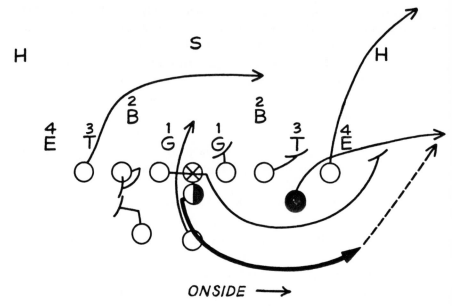

Figure 6–1. *The fullback trap pass vs. loose tackle six defense.*

The rules for the fullback trap pass:

> *Onside End*—Run "flag" pattern.
> *Onside Tackle*—Drive #2; if #2 is linebacker, drive #3.
> *Onside Guard*—Drive #1.
> *Center*—Drive #0, none there block #1 offside.
> *Off Guard*—Pull deep and block first man outside of onside offensive end.
> *Off Tackle*—Block first man on line of scrimmage outside of offside guard.
> *Off End*—Run "across" pattern.
> *Quarterback*—Reverse pivot and fake fullback trap, pull deep and execute run-pass option.
> *Fullback*—Fill over inside hip of left guard, faking fullback trap, get tackled.
> *Slotback*—Run a "flat" route. Get width quickly.
> *Tailback*—Step up and block first man outside the offensive end.
> NOTE: *"Flag" pattern*—end drives off line of scrimmage at outside

knee of defensive halfback, head fakes inside and breaks for flag.

"Across" pattern—end releases as if to go downfield to block, gets a depth of 6 to 8 yards and continues across field at that depth.

The action of the fullback should hold the linebackers as they play the fullback trap. This leaves the flat zone open. With the quarterback getting on the corner with an option either to run or pass, great stress is put on the corner defense. The quarterback and the pulling guard must be drilled together so that the quarterback will know how to get on the outside hip of the guard and in a position to read the guard's block. By design, the play is outside; but if the defensive end should come across the line of scrimmage and gain depth, the guard should drive him out, thus enabling the quarterback to cut inside, but still execute the run-pass option.

The reading of the defensive coverage is relatively simple. If the defensive sideback is beaten deep by the onside end, the pass should be thrown up and over the defender and the end should run for the ball. If not, the option to run the ball or pass to the slotback is executed by the quarterback. If the defensive corner is "soft," the quarterback runs; or if the slotback is open in the flat, he passes.

We depend heavily on the inside running of our fullback. The linebackers must be made to respect this inside threat. If they do, the flat becomes a vulnerable area and this pass play can put a dangerous runner in a position to catch a short pass with room to run in an open area. In addition, the onside end who is running the "flag" route is now in excellent position to "peelback" block. This combination makes the fullback trap pass a strong part of our offensive attack.

The Off-tackle Power Sweep Bootleg Pass

The misdirection or "bootleg" pass is one of the most effective plays in football. Not only does this type of play take advantage of a play action fake, but it also creates misdirection which could cause the defensive secondary to start their rotation in the wrong direction. This possibility, plus the effectiveness of the power play in holding the linebackers to stop the run, creates a situation in which the offense can make the "big play."

"Bootleg" added to the play call indicates that the pass is a misdirection pass and that pass protection is set up to the side opposite the call of the play. For example, when we run the off-tackle power sweep play to the right, the play is called "46." The 40 series is the power series, and the 6 indicates the hole we are to attack. To fake this play to the right and to have protection set up in order to throw to the off-side, we call "46 bootleg pass." "46" indicates the play to be faked; "bootleg" indicates that it is a play action pass to the side away from the 6 hole and indicates bootleg type protection.

The play we are faking in this case is diagrammed and discussed in the chapter on the Georgia running game. (See Chapter 1, Figure 1–25.)

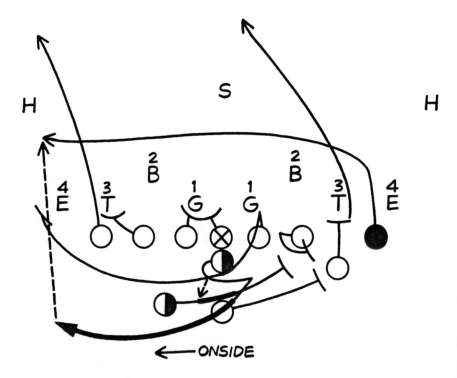

Figure 6–2. *The off-tackle power sweep bootleg pass vs. the loose tackle six defense.*

The rules for the off-tackle power sweep bootleg pass:

Onside End—Run "flag" pattern.
Onside Tackle—Drive #2; if #2 is linebacker, drive #3.
Onside Guard—Drive #1.

Center—Drive #0; none there, drive #1 offside.

Offside Guard—Pull and hook first man outside onside offensive end.

Offside Tackle—Drive #2; if #2 is a linebacker, you are responsible for blocking first man outside offside guard that rushes.

Offside End—Run an "across" pattern.

Quarterback—Reverse-pivot and toss ball to tailback, take a lead step as if to lead block but pivot and take inside handoff from tailback. Attack the corner with run-pass option.

Fullback—Block #4 offside.

Slotback—Block anyone in slot—then run pattern deep through the safety man.

Tailback—Receive the pitch as if to run power sweep, but hand inside to quarterback and continue to fake power play.

The power off tackle play is the "bread and butter" running play in the tight slot running offense. It is the play that can be called in any and all situations and at any place on the field. It is used in clutch situations where we must make the yardage. It is used going in for the score and also coming out from our own goal line. It must be successful. Therefore, the defense must play to stop this part of our attack to the slot on the strong side. For this reason, it is an ideal play from which to design a misdirection pass.

After the quarterback has tossed the ball to the tailback, he should complete his pivot and move as if to lead the power play. As a coaching point, we ask him to be sure that the defensive sideback whom we are attacking with the pass is able to see the numbers on the back of his jersey. Then he pivots and receives an inside handoff from the tailback, picks up the pulling guard who will attack the end, and then runs for the corner with the option to run or pass. Usually the onside end will take the defensive sideback deep with him as he runs the flag pattern, and the crossing end will be open as he runs his crossing route. If the quarterback elects to run, both the onside and the offside end are in excellent positions to "peelback" block; therefore, the play should be equally effective as a run or as a pass.

If the safety man should read the play and try to support the weak side defensive sideback, the slotback, after insuring the slot area, runs a "post" route through the safety man's area and has the opportunity for the "home run," if the safety has left that zone open. Should the quarterback elect to throw to the slotback, he will have to pull up and get set in order to make this throw which will be back to his inside.

The Wide Power Sweep Pass

The running play that is complemented with this play pass is illustrated and diagrammed in Chapter 1. (See Figure 1–27.)

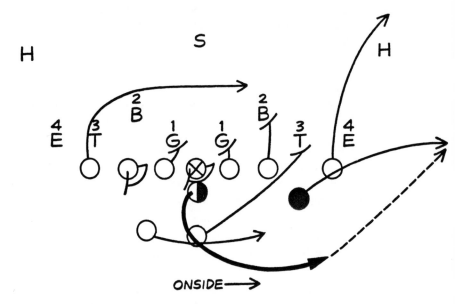

Figure 6–3. *The wide power sweep pass vs. the loose tackle six defense.*

The rules for the wide power sweep pass:

Onside End—Release and run "flag" pattern.
Onside Tackle—Drive #2.
Onside Guard—Drive #1.
Center—Drive #0; none there, drop-step for first man to show from offside.
Offside Guard—Drive #1; if #1 is linebacker, drop-step and protect offside.
Offside Tackle—Drive #2; if #2 is linebacker, step up and then drop-step to insure offside areas.
Offside End—Run "across" pattern.
Quarterback—Reverse pivot and hand-fake to tailback, roll out and execute run-pass option.

Fullback—Block #3.

Slotback—Run "flat" route.

Tailback—Quick motion and block #4 after faking with quarter-back.

NOTE: "Flat" route is the route run into the flat pass zone gaining width fast, but not more than 5 to 7 yards in depth.

The power sweep pass is designed to flood a zone and to put a receiver into the flat quickly in much the same manner as the quarterback sprint out pass. In this case, the quarterback will hand-fake to the tailback and then roll out on the corner. It is an option run or pass, but in this case it is usually a pass to the slotback in the flat.

The wide power sweep pass should be called when a tough rush is used to stop the power sweep or off-tackle play and when the linebacker "cheats" up to jam the hole. When the linebacker is in a position to do this, we feel that he cannot adequately cover the flat since he is forced by the play action fake to play the run first and the pass second. In this case, the ball will be thrown immediately after the hand-fake to the tailback just as the slotback breaks into the flat. The slotback works more for width than depth and the onside end will clear the zone by running a flag pattern which should eliminate the defensive sideback.

When facing a monster type defense, the use of the off-tackle power sweep or the wide power sweep will force the monster to play on the line of scrimmage. The linebacker should be too far removed to adequately cover the flat. Against the monster defense, the fullback will block the defensive end; and the tailback, after faking with the quarterback, will attack the monster man as indicated in the play rules above.

The combination of the off-tackle power sweep, the off-tackle power sweep bootleg pass, the wide power sweep, and the wide power sweep pass complement each other and have a high degree of consistency. This consistency is the factor we feel essential for the success of the ball control type game.

The Outside Belly Bootleg Pass

The running play that is complemented by the play action pass is illustrated and diagrammed in Chapter 1. (See Figure 1–38.)

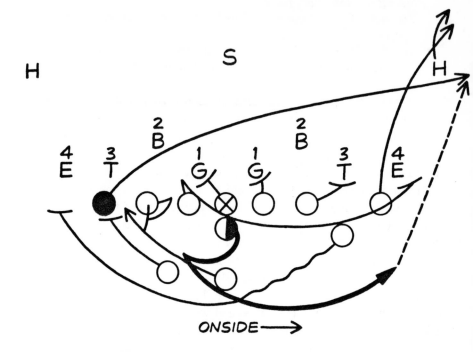

Figure 6–4. *The outside belly bootleg pass vs. the loose tackle six defense.*

The bootleg protection for this pass is the same as that described previously for the off-tackle power sweep bootleg pass. Remember, if a bootleg pass is called, the onside will be opposite to the side on which the play begins.

The rules for the outside belly bootleg pass are these:

> *Quarterback*—Reverse pivot and ride fullback into line of scrimmage, then pull ball and attack the corner with the run-pass option.
>
> *Fullback*—Fake belly off-tackle play.
>
> *Slotback*—Fly and block #4 offside.
>
> *Tailback*—Drive #3 offside.
>
> *Onside End*—Run "flag" route.
>
> *Offside End*—Run "hidden" route.
>
> NOTE: "Hidden" route is a pattern whereby the end goes inside the linebacker staying as close to the line of scrimmage as possible

in order to be "hidden," and then he breaks into the flat area gaining ground through the area vacated by the defensive halfback.

The outside belly series with the fullback off-tackle play and the belly option play have been sound plays in our ground attack, and for this reason they have proven to be a good basis for a misdirection bootleg pass. The slotback in this series of plays will go in motion away from the slot formation. In our terminology this is called "fly." By "flying" the slotback and having the quarterback ride the fullback into the line of scrimmage, the defense is forced to start its rotation. At the same time, the fake of the fullback into the line of scrimmage will hold the line-backers in close. The fullback should drive into the off-tackle hole, and if the execution of this fake is good, he should be tackled. After a good ride, the quarterback will pull the ball out, reverse his field, and attack the corner, reading the block of the pulling guard as described earlier in the off-tackle power sweep bootleg pass.

The onside end should run a flag route in order to take the defensive sideback with him deep. The offside end runs the hidden route, and should, by hugging the line of scrimmage, be able to break into an open area created by the sideback who has left this area to cover the deep outside zone. Utilizing his pulling guard, the quarterback executes the run-pass option.

We would like to have a play action pass for every major play in our offense. From game to game, much thought is given to the idea of beating a particular defensive adjustment or a particular defensive man who may be overly aggressive or unusually cautious. Special plays, especially play action passes, provide a great boost to the offense and serve to keep the defense off balance when they have been drilled through defensive recognition to stop a particular running play.

It is important that these pass plays be used in the proper situation if they are to be effective. This is a week-to-week decision to be made during the planning of the individual game plan. The ideal time to call the play action pass is on the nonpassing down, the short yardage situation, and the first down (especially if this follows a penalty against the defense, or if it is the first play after a changeover as a result of a fumble recovery or a pass interception). When the defense is geared to stop the run or when they might be overly aggressive is the ideal time for the play pass; used at this time, it can be the big play needed to change the complexion of the football game.

The Georgia running game must be consistent and strong if we are to maintain ball control. The same is true for the play action pass. Consistency is a must. When properly called and executed, the above plan will be consistent, and we believe it is not only "safe" for us but dangerous to the opposition.

The Sprint Out Passing Game

We have established the fact that we are a ball-control football team, and that the type of attack is determined by personnel. We have had excellent running quarterbacks.

To decide on the type of passing attack, first, it is necessary to decide on a basic offensive philosophy. In our offense we want the quarterback to run. This can be done with options, both split T and outside belly, with play action passes and bootleg passes, and with the sprint out pass and sprint out keep. Our most consistent outside play has been with the quarterback sprinting out and keeping. We believe that the sprint out pass with the option to run is the nearest thing to the halfback pass and that this puts great pressure on the defense.

The sprint out is run from tight and wide formations. This makes it necessary for the defense to make adjustments to our basic sprint out action plays. In addition to different sets, the patterns will also vary. Whenever possible we throw to a single receiver with the quarterback having an option to run. Finally, we will start our sprint out action and pull up to throw. This is basically the throwback pass, but we also throw to the onside, especially to a wide end or flanker, in order to attack certain coverages.

Above all, the basic objective on the sprint out is to afford us a way of getting the quarterback on the corner quickly with maximum blocking. The idea is to get a good running quarterback on the corner quickly, having the option either to run the ball or to pass. Actually there are two plays in the series. One is a precalled keep and the other is an option run or throw. The blocking rules for the keep are described in Chapter 1 (Figure 1–13), but some detailed explanation may help in understanding our plan of attacking the corner quickly and strongly.

From a tight slot formation, the loose six defense can be attacked as follows: (See Figure 6–5.)

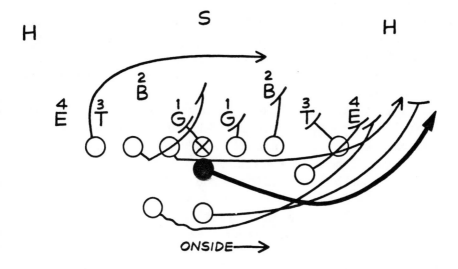

Figure 6–5. *The quarterback sprint keep vs. the loose tackle six defense.*

Strong end—Attack the tackle with a one-on-one butt block aiming for his inside hip. The inside hip is a couple of inches to the left of the belt buckle. This is a fine point, but we believe it gives our end a mental edge in taking away penetration by the defensive tackle stunting to the inside as we are "already there." At any rate, the end cannot allow penetration. The end starts the one-on-one block, and if the tackle goes down to the inside, the block becomes a reverse or wrong shoulder drive block with the head in front and the right forearm and elbow thrown high and tight into the side or rear of the defensive tackle. We use the defender's own momentum in taking him down the line of scrimmage.

Slotback—All plays from a tight slot for our slotback and end should appear to the defense as a double team block. The Georgia attack is ball control and the off tackle power sweep is the number one play, so the opponent must defend against it. The defense must be made to respect

152   HONOR THE RUN OR THROW

the off tackle play or the wide game will not be effective. Although the
power sweep and the sprint out keep actions are entirely different, we
believe and we sell our players on the fact that the opponent cannot
stop both of them, because these plays complement each other.

The slotback should lead step with his right foot, in this case, at the
center of the offensive end's tail, and he should attack the outside knee
of the defensive end with a one-on-one block which we call the "cut
block." The slotback must drive his head through and to the outside of
the defensive end's outside knee; then he must work upfield scrambling
on all fours.

Tailback—The tailback should be sent in one-count motion, which
puts him in a position to turn up the field and clean up the block of the
slotback. In effect, this is a double team block on the key defender on
the corner. If the slotback has successfully accomplished his block, the
tailback would become an additional lead blocker downfield.

Fullback—Our fullback has been exceptionally adept at the running
power block. He runs an arc as in the split T option and aims for the
defensive sideback. He will attack the sideback, depending on what the
defender decides to do. The quarterback attempts to get in the fullback's
hip pocket, forcing the defender to come through the fullback to make
the tackle; therefore, the fullback's block (either in or out) is determined
by the defensive sideback's move to make the tackle.

The following diagram will illustrate how the fullback makes his decision on the block.

Figure 6–6. *The fullback's path and block on the
quarterback sprint keep.*

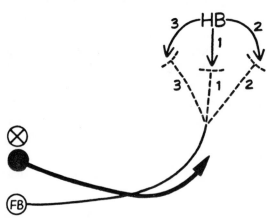

If the sideback stays in his original position, our fullback will attempt to run over him. (This is position #1.) If the sideback takes an angle to the outside, our fullback turns out on him and blocks out. (This is #2.) Should the defender try to force inside, the fullback turns in on him, and the quarterback is free outside. (This is #3.) The running power block has been exceptionally good for us.

The rest of the blocks are routine blocks for any type of sweep, so they will not be discussed except to say that the onside tackle must be very quick in order to execute a cutoff type block on the strong side linebacker. This block is described in the chapter on line play. (See Chapter 4, page 79.)

Quarterback—The quarterback should front out and get depth on the first step. We run him deep, and this gets him in a position to maneuver better. Also it will look more like the passes, both the sprint out and pull up types. He must get behind the fullback quickly, and the faster he gets to the corner, the better the play. For this play to be successful, a quarterback with the ability to run is essential.

We are a ball-control football team, and the quarterback sprint keep is one of our basic and most effective plays. To complement this play and to make our quarterbacks more effective and dangerous as runners, the sprint out pass is used.

The sprint out pass is an option run or pass play that puts great pressure on the corner and forces quick coverage in the flats. It is also a pass that can be thrown successfully by an average passer if a great deal of time is spent drilling him on reading the defensive coverage. A "soft" corner invites the run while a "tough" corner rush should result in the quarterback throwing the ball.

In order to use this play, you must have a good running quarterback who can read the coverage and make a decision. This decision, whether to run or pass, must be made on the run and without any hesitation. An average passer who is a good, intelligent runner will be able to put great pressure on the defense if he can correctly determine the coverage.

The rules for the sprint out pass are as follows:

Onside End—Release and run a "flag" route.
Onside Tackle—Drive #2; if #2 is a linebacker, reach #3.
Onside Guard—Drive #1.
Center—Drive #0. If no man is over you, fill and then drop-step, looking to the offside for the first man to show.

Off Guard—Drive #1. If #1 is a linebacker and does not come, step up and then drop-step. Block the first man to show.

Off Tackle—Drive #2; if #2 is a linebacker, step up and drop back to insure offside area.

Off End—Release and run a "bend-in" pattern.

Quarterback—Open at 45 degree angle, get depth and read the coverage. Use the fullback's block. Remember it is a run-pass option.

Fullback—Lead step parallel to line of scrimmage, block the first man to show outside of the offensive end.

Slotback—Run a quick "flat" route.

Tailback—Run a "swing" pattern.

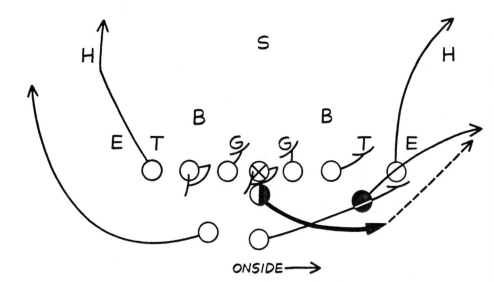

Figure 6–7. *The quarterback sprint out pass vs. the loose tackle six defense.*

The pass from a tight slot is best versus a three-deep secondary alignment. To attack the three-deep zone coverage, the slotback is expected to be able to outrun the strong side linebacker to the wide flat. This is the basic idea in attacking the zone.

The onside offensive end runs through the outside hip of the sideback, forcing the defender to cover him deep and to the outside. The slotback must make a wide, quick release to the flat, and he must not

become involved with the defensive end. He must get width as quickly
as possible—thus the idea of a footrace with the linebacker in what
should be a mismatch–slotback versus linebacker.

The fullback takes an almost parallel step and attacks the outside
knee of the corner defender—in this case, the defensive end. The hardest
thing to teach the fullback is to attack the end aggressively and turn
upfield to do so. Remember that this play is an option run or pass, and
if there is a "soft" defensive corner, the fullback becomes a lead blocker.
In order to be a lead blocker, he must attack the corner aggressively.

The quarterback gets depth quickly on the first step. He should carry
the ball in both hands about shoulder high, and he should have the
point of the ball down, not up, and already cocked.

As stated, the play is an option to run or throw, and to be specific,
the quarterback should react as follows:

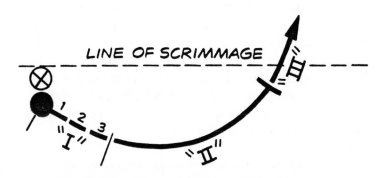

Figure 6–8. *Illustration showing path of the quar-*
terback on the sprint out pass.

It is a run for the first three steps as it takes a minimum of three
steps for the play to develop. Now the quarterback must be ready to
deliver the ball on this third step if the slotback is open. This is position
"I" in Figure 6–8. If the slotback is not open on this step, it becomes a
run-pass option with the right-handed passer being ready to throw each
time his left foot hits the ground until he reaches the line of scrimmage.
This is position "II" in the figure. When the quarterback reaches the line
of scrimmage, the option is over and the quarterback calls "Block" as
he becomes an open field runner. This is position "III."

If the quarterback understands this option, and if he knows his relationship to the line of scrimmage at all times, he will have some oppor-

tunities to go for the home run just as he reaches the line of scrimmage, because the defensive halfback on reading the quarterback may react up to support for the run too quickly. In this case, the end running the "flag" route would be open deep. The threat of the pass should be kept alive until the quarterback actually crosses the line of scrimmage.

The backside end should run a bend-in route, which is one of the best throwback patterns to help occupy the safety and backside defenders. The tailback will run a swing pattern to the backside. The quarterback will never attempt to throw to either of these receivers on the sprint out pass, but they will still occupy the defensive backs and help to prevent a quick secondary rotation. Running these patterns on the sprint out pass will also help to set them up when the throwback routes are called.

As an alternate route, the backside end can run an across route. He should get about 6 to 8 yards depth and come across into the area vacated by the strong side linebacker if the linebacker sprints to the flat to cover the slotback. If the flat and deep men are covered, the crossing end should break open. One precaution that must be taken is to be sure to drill the quarterback to square his shoulders to the flight of the ball and have good body balance and follow-through if he throws to the crossing end. Should the quarterback exercise the option to run, the crossing end should be in an excellent position to "peelback" block. The following figures will illustrate this alternate route both on the pass and on the run: (Figures 6–9 and 6–10.)

Figure 6–9. *The quarterback throwing to the crossing end on the sprint out pass.*

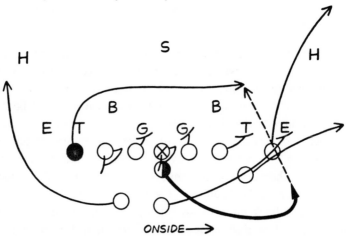

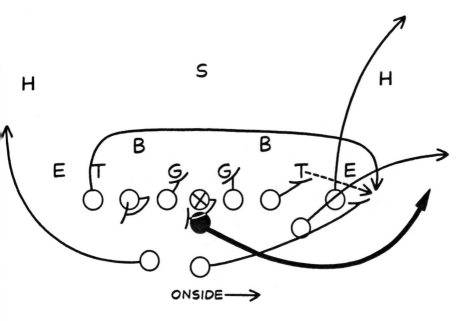

Figure 6–10. *The crossing end uses the "peelback" block on the sprint out pass with the quarterback keeping the ball.*

It must be emphasized to the quarterback that he should run the football when he encounters the "soft" defensive corner. He should not put the ball in the air unless the receiver is breaking wide open. As a coaching point, we tell the quarterback that he is never wrong if he does not throw even if a receiver is open. He must understand that he does not have to throw the ball on a called pass. He only throws when the receiver is definitely open. This takes the pressure off of the average passer and makes the decision his and only his. Should he elect to run when he should have thrown, he will be told about it but never scolded concerning the error. On the other hand, if he elects to pass when a receiver is not definitely open and when he should have run, this error will be discussed thoroughly. Our offensive goal is ball control, and therefore we must have consistency. This means no interceptions. The quarterback's simple rule is never to throw the ball if there is any doubt about the receiver's being open. If in doubt, run the ball.

A problem encountered in three-deep coverage is the "level off." (See Figure 6–11.)

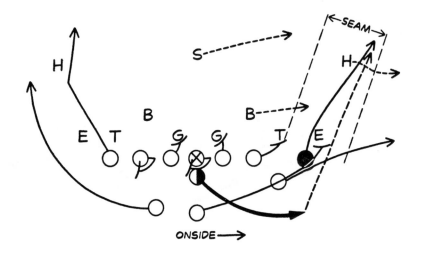

Figure 6–11. *The sprint out pass vs. the "level off" secondary coverage.*

"Level off" is a defensive maneuver designed to cover the flat. It puts the defensive sideback in excellent position to punish the receiver or to make the interception on the poorly thrown ball. However, the "seam" is open on the level off, and the onside end should be open and can be thrown to in this seam area before the safety can cover him.

The "seam" is the area between the sideback, who is leveling, and the safety, and is created by the level off of the sideback to the flat. Some teams will cheat the safety over to help cut down on this seam. When this is the case, the end should break to the sideline away from the safety as soon as he sees the sideback begin to level. By breaking toward the sideline, the end will increase the distance that the safety man must run in order to cover him. One precaution that should be taken is that the end should not cut too sharply toward the sideline because this action may make it possible for the sideback to cover him as he levels out and to the flat.

In reading this type of defensive coverage, if it is noted that the safety man cheats too much to the strong side, the quarterback should be ready to call a throwback pass to the offside and use a bend-in or hook route. (See this chapter, Figure 6–25.)

In attacking the monster defense with the monster on the line of scrimmage, the play becomes a definite pass and the ball must be thrown quickly as the corner will be "tough" with the defensive end and the monster forcing. (See Figure 6–12.)

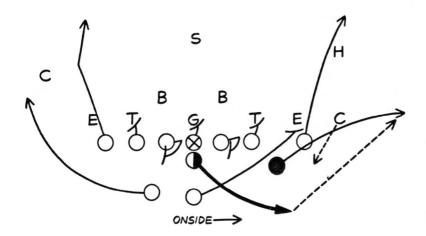

Figure 6–12. *The sprint out pass vs. the monster defense.*

To run these two plays—the quarterback keep or the sprint out pass—from a wide set, we use the wide slot I formation as indicated below: (See Figure 6–13.)

Figure 6–13. *The wide slot I formation.*

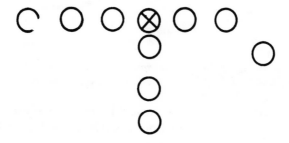

The basic goal is to get the running quarterback on the corner quickly. This formation also affords the offense an opportunity to double team on the corner without putting a back in motion. In other words, the idea is to have the tailback in a position to clean up on the corner or to become a lead blocker upfield for the quarterback if the slotback has made the block on the end. For a change of pace, the tailback may flare out of the backfield to the back side or he may be put in motion toward the formation or opposite the formation. These different maneuvers by the tailback will cause the defense to make different adjustments.

However, the main purpose is to attack the corner. If the defense has a soft corner, the quarterback runs. If the corner is tough, he should hit the flat quickly with the pass. The following diagram illustrates the pass from this formation. (See Figure 6–14.)

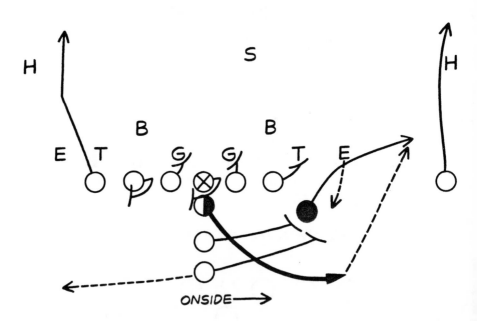

Figure 6–14. *The sprint out pass from the wide slot I formation vs. the loose tackle six defense.*

The split end runs a flag route, and his job is simply to make the wide defender cover him deep and outside. The defensive sideback must be taken deep.

The slotback must read the corner. If the defensive end is on the line of scrimmage in order to contain, he must release inside but get width to the flat as quickly as possible, exactly as described from the tight slot. He must outrun the linebacker to the flat and be ready to catch a quick pass. He must not get held up on the line of scrimmage. As soon as he makes the reception he becomes an open field runner. (See Figure 6–14.)

If the defensive end is in a walk-away position, and the defensive tackle has the containment assignment, the slotback must sprint upfield, staying inside the defensive end until he gets by the defensive end. Then he breaks flat to the sideline and sprints for it. (See Figure 6–15.) The quarterback with two lead blockers has the run-pass option. If the walk-away end covers the flat, the quarterback should run on the soft corner.

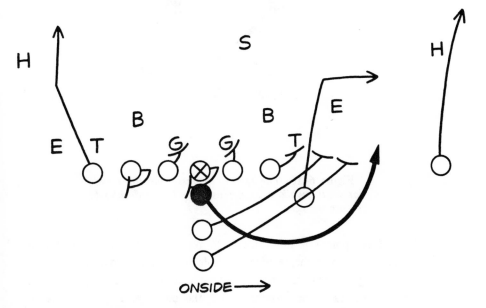

ONSIDE →

Figure 6–15. *The sprint out pass vs. the walk-away defensive end.*

If the walk-away defensive end decides to help contain the quarterback and attempts to come up to tackle him, the quarterback will exercise his option to throw and will pass to the slotback running open in the flat. (See Figure 6–16.)

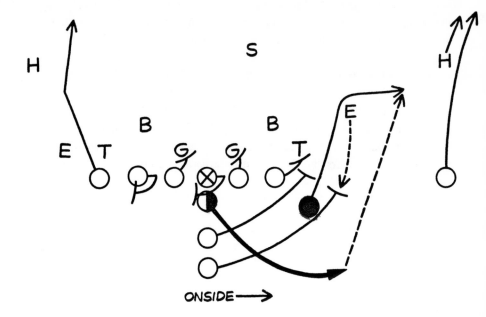

Figure 6–16. *The sprint out pass from the I wide slot vs. the walk-away defensive end who decides to contain the run.*

This development is not difficult to read, but it is imperative that both the passer and the receiver be able to read the coverage, and in this way they are able to anticipate what will take place. Repetition on the practice field is the answer. When the coverage is properly read, the play should be extremely effective and have a high degree of consistency.

This same line of thinking applies to the monster defense. If the monster is on the line of scrimmage in a forcing position, the ball must be thrown quickly because the protection may break down. In this case, the flat should be open. (See Figure 6–17.)

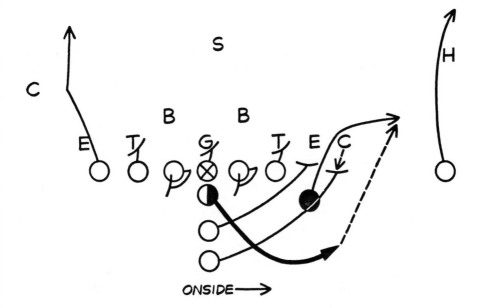

Figure 6–17. *The sprint out pass from the I wide slot vs. the monster defense with the monster on the line of scrimmage.*

If the monster is lined up in a walk-away position, attack him in exactly the same manner as that described for the loose tackle six defensive end in a walk-away position. (See Figure 6–18.)

Figure 6–18. *The sprint out pass from the I wide slot vs. the monster defense with the monster man in a walk-away position.*

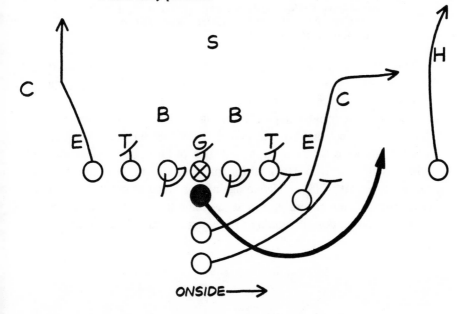

If the monster attempts to help with containment from his walk-away alignment, the play should become a pass. The slotback should run upfield until he gets by the monster man before he breaks toward the sideline.

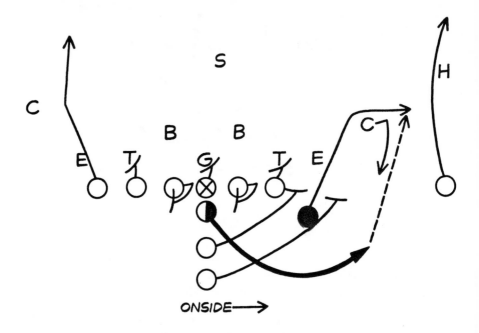

Figure 6–19. *The sprint out pass from the I wide slot vs. the monster defense with the monster man containing the run.*

Thus, the reading of the loose six defensive end and the monster man in a walk-away position are essentially the same. Reading the coverage is first in importance for both the passer and the receiver.

We vary the sprint out pass by using a "special" route we call the "turkey." We feel that we can combine the blocking principles of the quarterback keep with our sprint out idea of an option run or pass by using a single receiver. The goal for this special is to have our split end run a route that will be effective against any type of coverage, particularly man-for-man coverage, and at the same time have the quarterback exercising the option of running or passing the ball. (See Figures 6–20 and 6–21.)

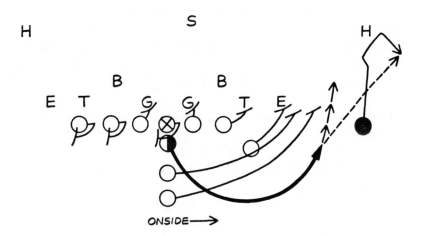

Figure 6–20. *The sprint out pass from the I wide slot with the offensive end running the "turkey" route vs. the loose tackle six defense.*

Figure 6–21. *The sprint out pass from the I wide slot with the offensive end running the "turkey" route vs. the monster defense.*

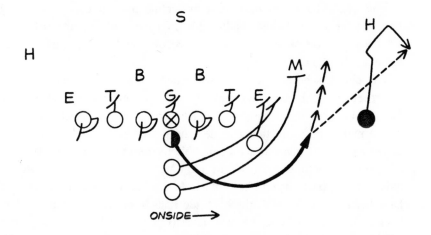

As seen in the previous play diagrams, we are able to put great pressure on the defensive corner using the wide slot I formation. We believe that the quarterback who is a good runner can cause the defense much trouble with the strong blocking power we are able to concentrate on the corner, utilizing the fullback, the tailback, and the slotback.

The "turkey" route is designed to defeat man-to-man coverage and is one that is not a time cut as is the usual "out" pattern. It is also an optional pass route in that it may become a deep flag route should the end be able to beat the defender deep, or it will be an "out" cut if the defender will not allow the end to get deep on him. We want the defender to perform his job, which is not letting us get behind him. If he does this perfectly, we should be able to get open on the out cut since the route calls for the end to break out and back toward the line of scrimmage.

To accomplish the "turkey" route, the end will have to make three moves. The first will be a good head fake to the inside while running under control. The end will then break for the flag and sprint trying to beat the sideback deep and to the outside. Should he be successful he will continue to run, and the quarterback will deliver the ball high and to the outside leading the receiver. If the defender does his job, he will not allow the end to beat him deep, but he will be forced to turn his body to the outside and run. At this point, when the sideback has been forced to turn and run, the end will break out and back toward the line of scrimmage and receive the ball as he makes this out cut.

The quarterback has maximum protection and should be sprinting hard on the corner while reading his offensive end and the defensive sideback. His throw will be timed by reading and anticipating the out cut made by the end.

The play has been most successful when going for the first down, as the receiver simply does not make his out cut and come back for the ball until he has the necessary yardage. This is made possible because of the maximum protection afforded the passer by having only one receiver and by the quarterback being able to run until he reaches the line of scrimmage before he throws. In addition to the regular protection, we have kept the backside end in to block on third down pass situations, and have been able to prevent the backside rush from catching the quarterback from behind should the pass have to be thrown late.

Thus, with nine players involved in pass protection, we have an advantage for the run as well as the time needed to execute the proper pass route at the depth needed for the first down.

As a coaching point, it should be stated that we would like this play to be an option. The first option is to run. The second option is to pass. The receiver is usually able to get open, and oftentimes the quarterback will throw when he could have run for good yardage. The quarterback should run when he has made the corner. The principle of ground control offense is consistency. When yardage can be had simply by running, do not risk throwing. On the other hand, with the opponent thinking of you as a running team, the pass can be a great weapon.

The sprint out passing game may be broken down into four phases. In the order of their importance, we believe them to be these:

1. Pass protection
2. Recognition of the defensive coverage
3. The passer
4. The receiver

The skill of the passer himself will determine the style of play—dropback, sprint out, or play action, but in any passing game regardless of how great the passer is or the receivers are, the first necessity is being able to protect and then being able to recognize and attack the coverage. Proper execution requires a great deal of work and repetition in practice.

The Throwback Pass

The throwback pass is designed to cut down on pursuing linebackers and to prevent the defensive secondary from rotating too quickly.

Every attempt must be made to start the throwback action exactly as the quarterback sprint out pass. The quarterback must be schooled and drilled daily in order to accomplish this. The defense is taught to read the throwback action; therefore, the offense must counter by making all plays in the sprint out and throwback series start alike.

As the quarterback starts his sprint in the throwback, he must gain depth but look to the onside flat as if reading the corner defense. When he comes to the "4" or "5" station, which is behind the offensive tackle, he should pull up and immediately look to the backside hook and be ready to throw the ball. (See Figure 6–22.)

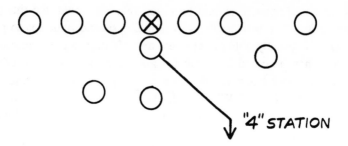

Figure 6–22. *The quarterback action on the throw-back pass.*

The basic play in the throwback series is called the 4 or 5 pass. Against a loose tackle six defense with a three-deep it would run as follows: (See Figure 6–23.)

Figure 6–23. *The basic throwback pattern (4) vs. the loose tackle six defense.*

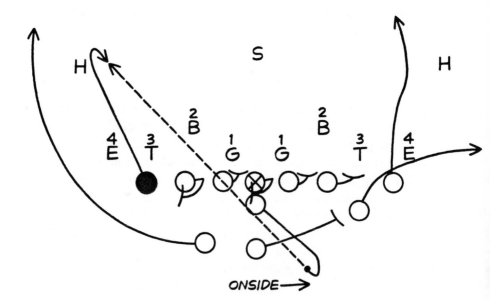

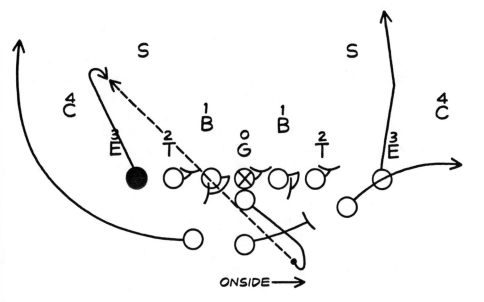

Figure 6–24. *The basic throwback pattern vs. the
5–2 defense.*

The rules for the throwback pass:

Onside End—Release and run a "bend-in" route.
Onside Tackle—Block #2; if #2 is a linebacker, block #3.
Onside Guard—Block #1; if #1 is a linebacker, insure the area.
Center—Block #0. If no one over you, drop-step, look to offside
and block first man to show.
Offside Guard—Block #1. If #1 is linebacker and does not rush,
fill and then drop-step, look to offside and block first man to show.
Offside Tackle—Block #2. If #2 is a linebacker, fill and then drop-
step to insure the offside area.
Offside End—Release and run a "hook" route. (*Coaching point:*
As soon as you hook, locate and read the linebacker—slide to an
open area.)
Quarterback—Open with the right foot and get depth quickly. Set
up 7 yards behind the onside tackle. "Read the coverage."
Fullback—Block the first man to show outside the onside offensive
end.
Slotback—Run a "flat" route.
Left Half—Run a "swing" route.

As the quarterback pulls up, he brings the ball up and gets set to throw. He must immediately "read the defensive coverage." In this case, he should read the backside linebacker. If the linebacker has started with the flow and pulls up as the quarterback pulls up, the end should be open immediately and the ball must be thrown quickly. If the linebacker is covering the backside hook zone, the end should slide to an open area, and the quarterback should deliver the ball as soon as the end gets open.

As mentioned in the discussion on the sprint out pass, timing is the all-important factor in successful passing. This is especially true on the throwback hook. Much time must be spent to coordinate the time it takes the quarterback to set up with the depth of the end's hook route in order to be sure the receiver is ready for the ball when the quarterback is ready to throw.

Depending on the individual end's speed, his hook route will vary from 9 to 13 yards from the line of scrimmage.

If the sprint out pass can be established as a major weapon in the attack, the defense may "level off" to the formation side. Should this occur, the throwback "bend-in" route should be an excellent route. (See Figure 6–25.)

Figure 6–25. *The throwback bend-in pattern (4 "bend-in") vs. the loose tackle 6 defense with the defensive secondary "leveling off."*

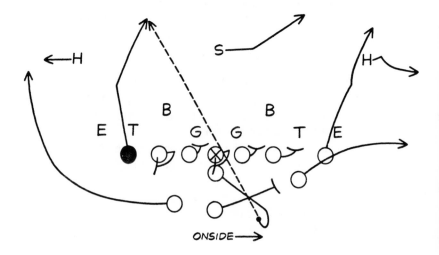

If the defensive halfback should overplay the hook pattern or the bend-in, the "swing" route by the halfback can become a big play. In this case, the quarterback must read the coverage and hit the swing man on time. (See Figure 6–26.)

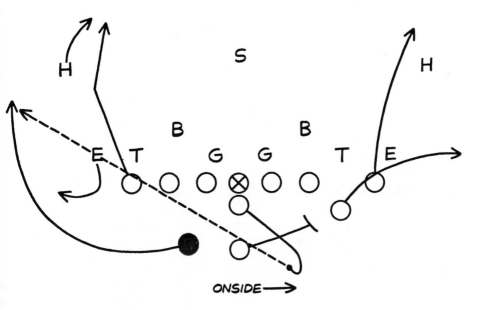

Figure 6–26. *The throwback hook with the defensive halfback overplaying the end on his "bend-in" route. This is shown vs. the loose tackle six defense.*

Probably the most consistent and safest of the throwback patterns is the "delay" route by the end. In this route, the end sets up as if to block in the pass protection. He then reads the linebacker. If the linebacker drives back to the hook zone, the end should slip inside of him and catch the ball down the middle. (See Figure 6–27.)

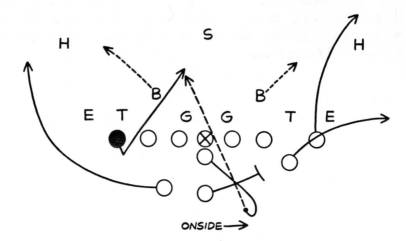

Figure 6–27. *The throwback pass with the end running a "delay" route vs. the loose tackle six defense with the linebacker covering the hook zone.*

If the linebacker plays the flow and then the backside hook, the offensive end should go straight upfield and catch the ball over his inside shoulder. (See Figure 6–28.)

Figure 6–28. *The throwback pass with the end running a delay route vs. the 5–2 defense with the linebacker flowing and then reacting toward the hook zone.*

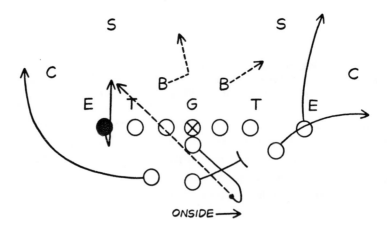

When throwing against man-to-man pass defense, it is best to create a mismatch. For example, when a linebacker is assigned to cover the tailback, there is an excellent chance of hitting the "swing" route because the tailback may be faster than the linebacker, and therefore, be able to get open. (See Figure 6–29.)

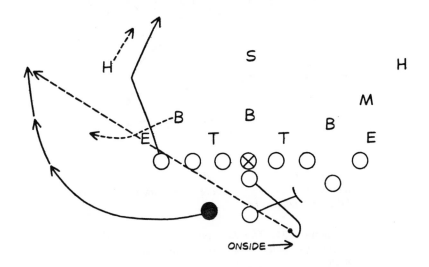

Figure 6–29. *The throwback pass with the tailback running a "swing" pattern vs. man-to-man pass defense.*

When throwing back, as with other types of passing, protection is the number one problem. Therefore, it is important to have a plan of protection to take care of blitzing linebackers or a strong corner rush with the monster man rushing.

This type rush is handled by calling "solid" protection. Solid protection keeps the halfback on the onside of the play in on the pass protection plan, and he is assigned the #3 defender. Now the fullback blocks #4, and the protection is deployed so that we can handle a four-man rush on the onside. (See Figures 6–30 and 6–31.)

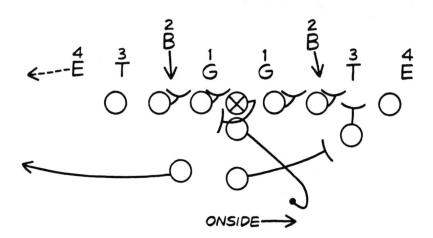

Figure 6–30. *The throwback pass with solid protection (4 "solid") vs. loose tackle six defense with blitzing linebackers.*

Figure 6–31. *The throwback pass with "solid" protection (4 "solid") vs. monster defense using eight-man rush.*

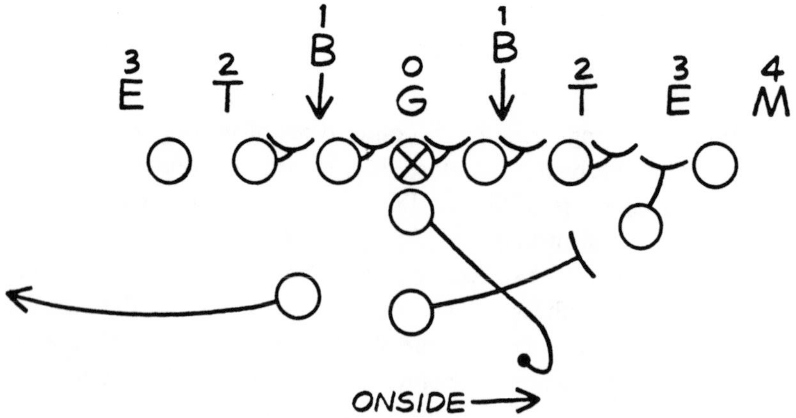

The solid pass protection rules are as follows:

Onside End—Release and run pattern.
Onside Tackle—Block #2.
Onside Guard—Block #1.
Center—Block #0. If none there, fill and drop-step. Look to offside and block first man to rush.
Offside Guard—Block #1. If #1 is a linebacker and does not come, fill and then drop-step; look to offside and block first man to rush.
Offside Tackle—Block #2. If #2 is a linebacker, step up and drop-step to insure offside area.
Offside End—Release and run pattern.
Onside Halfback—Block #3.
Fullback—Block #4.

In addition to the above protection scheme, it is also possible to use "solid" protection and keep the offside end in a block. Now the idea will be to throw to the onside of the formation, usually to one receiver such as a split end. For example, the play could be "4 solid right end out," and the protection would be as follows: (See Figure 6–32.)

Figure 6–32. *The throwback pass using "solid" protection (4 "solid") vs. loose tackle six defense, with the backside end being kept in to block.*

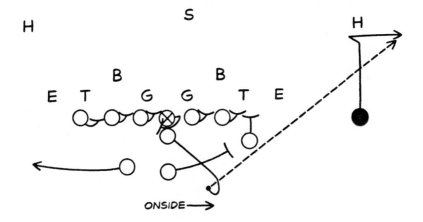

This type pull up pass complements the sprint out passing series, and by using the proper protection combinations, it is possible to afford the quarterback time to throw a time cut route.

The throwback pass will accomplish the following:

1. Cut down on quick pursuit.
2. Delay the quick secondary rotation.
3. Afford an opportunity for a mismatch in attacking man-to-man coverage.
4. Give the passing attack a good change of pace.

The two most important areas of work offensively are:

1. Make the throwback pass look like the sprint out pass.
2. Be sure to throw on time. A late throw on this pass is extremely susceptible to interception.

In the preparations made for each game, we construct an offensive game plan that will, hopefully, enable us to score enough points so that we can win the football game.

The offensive plan for each game is a separate, new game plan regardless of the opposition. Oftentimes there will be many of the same plays included in each plan. We feel, as most offensive coaches do, that we carry entirely too much offense because we never use all of the plays in a single game. But, when we consider the many defensive alignments that a team has to face, we feel it would be better to carry a surplus of plays in the event situations during the course dictate their use.

Planning for a football game is a race against the clock. There are only seven days between games. The earlier a coaching staff can finalize its game plan, the longer it will have to teach it to the players. The longer a team can work on a certain game plan the more proficient it will become in

Devising the Game Plan for Ball-Control Offense

its execution and the greater will be the chances of winning the game.

All of this theory is, of course, based upon having the "right" game plan. And how does a team go about having the right game plan? There is no sure way to predetermine the merits of a game plan, but there are a couple of prerequisites that must be present before a sound game can be formulated. They are these: (1) an offensive coaching staff must have a thorough knowledge of the opposition, and (2) the offensive staff must be able to judge each week the capabilities of its own offensive personnel, in light of the opposition that they will be facing.

In order to have a thorough knowledge of the opposition, they must be scouted thoroughly. This scouting begins before the football season when each assistant coach is assigned to scout a team that we will play. During the spring, this coach studies films that he has borrowed and if possible watches the team's spring football game. This will allow him an opportunity to become acquainted with the team's general plan and its personnel. Also, while making these evaluations the coach should be putting together some suggestions, such as plays, etc., that might be useful when the actual game week arrives in the fall.

During the football season the scouting coach should scout the team at least three times, taking a play-by-play account of the team's defensive plays. If possible, other films might be viewed in order to add to the play-by-play accounts he has already taken. On the first day (Sunday for us) of the week of his game, he should have the following information ready to present to the offensive coaching staff:

1. A specific evaluation of the defensive personnel of the team that we play next, including the team's conditioning, its size and speed, its better players, its average players, and any other information pertinent to personnel.
2. The major defense that the team uses plus its adjustments to offensive sets that we use or can use.
3. The long yardage defense or passing down defenses employed by the team plus adjustments and pass coverage (zone or man-to-man). This information should include the following: (a) the team's long yardage pressure defenses or blitzes, and (b) the team's long yardage "contain" defenses.
4. The opposition's short yardage defense or defenses.
5. The opposition's goal line defense or defenses.

Based on the play-by-play accounts that have been accumulated on the opposition, we should be able to detect some tendencies on their part to use certain of their defenses in certain field positions, certain down and distance situations, and in certain time situations.

Armed with the above information, the offensive coaching staff begins to devise an offensive game plan. The first step is to choose one or two offensive formations to use. This selection is made on this basis: (1) the ability of the offensive formation to allow the offensive staff to get the highest and best use of its personnel, with respect to the plays that can be run from the formation, and (2) the adjustments likely to be used against these sets and the seeming vulnerability of these adjustments to certain offensive plays.

After an offensive formation has been chosen, the first step is to devise a strong inside attack. This attack is built around counterplays, isolation plays, and trap plays. These plays should present balance and strength and will serve to keep the opposition's defense in tight and "at home."

Once the inside attack has been settled on, we next devise the off tackle and wide game. We feel like we can make good yardage running the ball inside, but as the defense crowds the inside attack it will become necessary to go wide to loosen the defense up. Also, experience has shown us that it is usually the wide plays that are the long gainers and eventually the touchdown producers. We usually install an option type play plus a power sweep type play so that we can go wide in more than one way.

After the basic running attack has been decided on, and all blocking situations have been thoroughly reviewed, we install our basic passing game utilizing play action passes, bootleg passes, sprint out passes, and throwback type passes.

This basic part of the planning is completed by Tuesday so that we can work on it at this time (Monday having been a review and loosening up day for us).

On Tuesday we devise our short yardage and goal line attack. The short yardage and goal line attack is crucial. It must not fail. Long hours are spent hashing out the merits of certain plays and the ability of certain players in order to come up with the best possible attack. We usually decide on one or two plays that are designed to make from 1 to 3 yards and one or two plays that are designed to make 1 yard or less.

This short yardage and goal line plan is taught to the offensive team on Wednesday along with a review of the basic running and passing attack.

On Wednesday, the offensive coaching staff begins work on the "specials" or razzle-dazzle plays as some are prone to call them. We usually design a wide running "special" play such as the one diagrammed in Figure 7–1 that we used to score the winning touchdown in a crucial game.

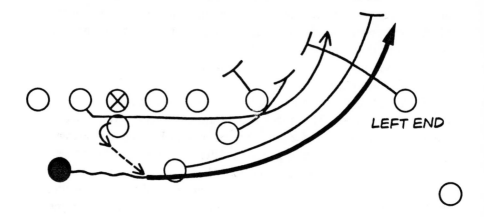

Figure 7–1. *The special wide power sweep.*

After we have devised a special wide play, we then devise a special pass to be used in conjunction with our regular passing game. The special pass diagrammed in Figure 7–2 was used to score a 70-yard touchdown that enabled us to upset a team in an opening game.

Figure 7–2. *The "special" lateral pass.*

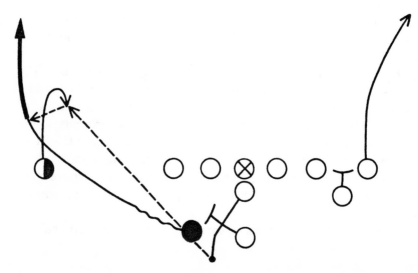

We also devise a special type pass to use in the short yardage situations when we detect from the scouting report that a team gambles on short yardage in order to stop the run. The play diagrammed in Figure 7–3 was used to score a 60-yard touchdown in a short yardage situation.

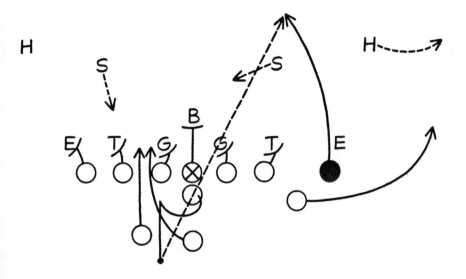

Figure 7–3. *A special short yardage pass.*

The team receives a comprehensive written scout report early in the week. A player must study this scout report in order to play as best he can on Saturday. In addition, a written assignment sheet that includes pertinent coaching reminders is given out so that a player can sharpen his knowledge of assignments relative to the upcoming game.

On Thursday, the entire game plan is rehearsed in the team period against dummies. On this day, we start out at our own goal line employing the plays that we will use in this danger zone and running them against the opposition's pressure defense. We then work our way out to the full offense zone where we can run any play in the game plan. We alternate field position from hash mark to hash mark. We progress on down the field to the four down zone (inside the opposition's 35 yard line). At this point, we rehearse our four down offensive plan.

Later, in the team period, we go over our short yardage and goal line plan.

After we have rehearsed all of our basic offense, we will work on all of our "special" plays to make sure that we are clear on them. These plays are usually "bench" calls; that is, the quarterbacks are instructed not to use them until word is sent in from the bench to do so.

After the regular offense and the special offense has been drilled upon, we will work on our two-minute offense. This is the offense that we use right before the half or at the end of the game. We work on this by giving a ball to our offensive team and then let them move the ball down the field in two minutes or less.

On Thursday, the game plan is diagrammed and copies are made in preparation for the final quarterback meetings. (See Figure 7–4 for a sample game plan.)

Figure 7–4. *A sample game plan.*

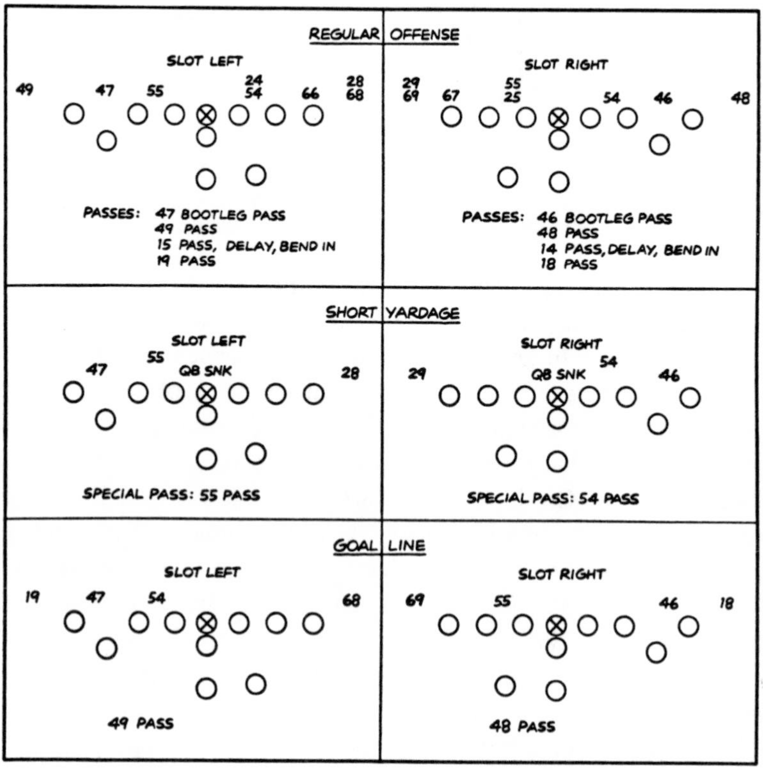

The final quarterback meetings are held on the day before the game and on the morning of the game. The offensive coaches can make all the decisions they want to concerning hypothetical game situations, but once the game gets under way the execution of the game plan rests in the hands of the quarterback. Therefore, the quarterback must be schooled to understand the game plan, and he must be made to understand the basic thinking behind the formulation of the overall game plan.

Throughout the week the quarterback must be kept up to date on the progress of the game plan as it is devised. He must know the reasons for the offensive sets that have been installed; he must know the reasons behind the plays that have been devised; he must know about the strengths and weaknesses of the opposition's defense; and he should know the blocking assignments of his offensive teammates so that he can encourage specific men on certain plays. In short, he should have a working knowledge of the entire offense if he is to be entrusted with calling plays.

In the final quarterback meetings, the quarterback should be given a game plan and a field map whereon he should write the plays to use in the various areas. He should be schooled on plays that set up certain plays and familiarized with the plays to use in various short yardage and goal line situations, passing situations, etc.

After the quarterback has had a day to study the total game plan, he should be reviewed on the morning of the game in order to rehearse the game plan and to get his thinking straight on certain situations relevant to the game.

If the quarterback understands the merits of the game plan and he has had the proper training concerning the multitude of variables that he must consider in the minute-to-minute progress of the football game, he will call a sound game.

The kicking game—the punt, punt return, kickoff, kickoff returns, and extra point and field goal situations—represents about 25 per cent of a football game. Since it represents so much of the total game, both the coaching staff and the players must be convinced that all phases of the kicking game are vitally important. We work on the kicking game every day, including it in our specialty period and in our team periods in order to emphasize its importance to our players.

Our practices begin each day with a 15-minute specialty period. (See Chapter 2.) Staff members are assigned to the various kicking groups in order that each group might be closely supervised during this time. The centers, punters, and punt receivers work together in one group. The centers, holders, and place-kickers work in another group on extra points and field goals, while the kickoff men work together in another group.

The offensive centers rotate from one group to

8

The Kicking Game as the Winning Edge

185

another so that they can work on both the long and short snaps.

Prior to our team period each day, we have a ten-minute team kicking period in which the offensive team and the defensive team work on their respective segments of the kicking game.

The Punting Game

The offense gains an advantage once it gets inside the opposition's 35 yard line. This area is known as the four down zone because the offense can now use all four downs in order to make a first down. Good defense and a sound punting game play a vital role in helping an offensive team get to the four down area. There are few offensive plays that will gross 35 to 40 yards as consistently as a punt. If the defense can force the opposition to punt back after two or three plays, and our punting game is better than the opponent's punting game, we should have gained yardage on the punt exchange. Thus, through the exchanging of punts a superior kicking game will enable a team to progress toward the opponent's goal.

The important aspects of the punting game include these: (1) protection, (2) the punt coverage, and (3) the kicking of the ball.

(1) The Punt Protection: Our normal spread punt alignment is the basic seven-man spread punt utilizing two "up backs" who are lined up between the center and the guards. (See Figure 8–1.)

Our linemen line up in a two-point stance with their toes on a line with the heel of the center. This type of lineup gets the linemen further away from the defenders. This gives them time to get better prepared to protect.

Figure 8–1. *The 7–2 spread punt.*

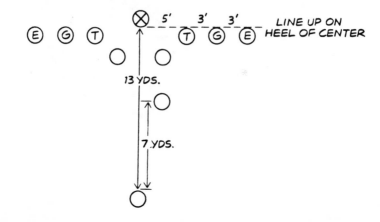

The protection rules for the 7–2 spread punt are these:

CENTER: First assignment is to make a good snap. Blocks man over or fills for overload. If no overload in gap or stack, release and cover. Snaps ball when ready after *deep back* has given command "set."

TACKLES: Lines up elbows on knees next to center. This gives our larger men a chance to protect the middle zone and gives us more outside speed from our guards. The first move is to drop-step to outside keeping the inside foot in place—slams to the outside. Never let two men shoulder to shoulder on up back. Cover.

GUARDS: Lines up elbows on knees next to tackles. Drop-steps to outside keeping inside foot in place. Slams to the outside. Cuts split down if there are two men in gap inside or if one is inside and one is head up—cover fast and contain.

END: Lines up elbows on knees next to guards. Drop-steps to outside keeping inside foot in place. Slams to outside. Cuts split down if there are two men in gap inside or if one inside or head up. Covers and contains.

UP BACK: Elbows on knees. This allows player to see better. Lines up in gap between center and tackles. On snap steps up into the hole with inside foot and blocks in area. If no one is in the hole area or in the cross charge position, releases through area and goes for ball.

DEEPBACK OR SEARCHLIGHT: Lines up 7 yards from kicker making sure not to give ground. Blocks first man to show in kicking area. Covers right and plays as a safety. Looks for an overloaded side. Gives a command of "set" when all players are ready.

KICKER: Lines up 13 yards from ball. Kicks and covers left side as safety.

(2) **The Punt Coverage:** Good, aggressive punt coverage is a must in order to have a sound punting game. It is necessary to have a group of athletes who want to win in order to get good coverage. Good position is necessary, but tackling the punt returners is the most important aspect. (See Figure 8–2 for illustration of punt coverage.)

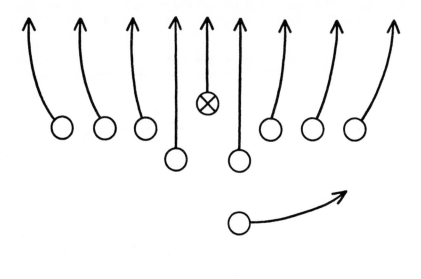

Figure 8–2. *Punt coverage from the 7–2 spread punt.*

The coaching points for the 7–2 spread punt and coverage are as follows:

1. Keep head up and eyes open
2. Slam hard
3. Hold block for count of thousand and one. (Name of game is hit and sprint.)
4. Release quick and cover
5. We ask all men to sprint until they hear thump of ball, take quick look, find ball, sprint hard, and get under control just before driving through ballcarrier.
6. Punish ballcarrier.

(3) The Kicking of the Ball: Looking at positions and personnel, we feel that the *center* is the most important person in the kicking game. He is asked to make a perfect snap in .6 to .8 of a second, be able to block from an awkward position, and also be able to cover and tackle. Much work should be done in developing the snapper.

See Chapter 4 page 70 for further description and discussion of the center's long snap techniques and drills.

The punter is the second most important man on the punting team. It is important that he be able to kick high and far. Also, he should have presence of mind so that he can make the best of bad snaps and other unexpected developments.

Too much emphasis has been placed on overcoaching the kicker. Occasionally this could be a threat; however, we feel that a staff member should be assigned to the kicker in order to detect and point out any flaws the kicker might not be able to see in himself.

The following are coaching tips pertinent to training the punter:

(1) Make sure the punter loosens up well before he begins kicking. Running and stretching exercises should be stressed.

(2) Dropping the ball should be done with the front point slightly down and slightly turned to the inside.

(3) The kicker's hands should be placed on the side of the ball and released simultaneously in order to get a correct drop. The right hand should be placed on the side toward the rear of the ball and the left hand on the left side slightly forward.

(4) Always be sure that the kicker turns his kicking toe down plus moving toes and entire foot forward in shoe just before the snap.

(5) The punter should look the ball in from the center—never taking eyes off the ball.

(6) The punter should be careful not to overstride.

(7) The punter should stand in a relaxed position, with his knees bent slightly, and his arms and hands extended but relaxed. His feet should be only 6 to 8 inches apart, with his kicking foot slightly forward. This gives the kicker a short step first with lead foot, then a full step with the left foot, and then kick the ball with the right foot. Do not take eyes off the ball until it has been kicked.

(8) The kicker should get ball off within two seconds after snap, always striving for an improvement on time.

(9) Good leg follow-through is essential.

(10) If you have a boy who is a natural, and he takes three steps or drops ball differently, move him back one step but don't change his method.

Do not expect your punter to react under adverse conditions unless you have drilled him in similar situations on the practice field.

The following are some special situations for the punter that should be rehearsed in football practice:

(1) Kicking into the wind—use a lower release which will help the ball to remain lower and the wind will not have as much effect.

(2) Kicking a wet ball.

(3) Bad snap on third down—run if there is a danger of a blocked kick, because you still have another down.

(4) Practice kicking out-of-bounds. Place markers on sideline and after receiving ball turn and kick straight through as you would normally.

(5) Kicking a short, high ball to be grounded inside your opponent's 10 yard line.

The Tight Punt

There are times when an offensive football team has to sacrifice good punt coverage in order to insure that the punt is gotten off, and that the punt will not be blocked.

When a team is backed up near its own goal and there is not room for the normal spread punt, then the tight punt can be used. In the tight punt formation (see Figure 8–3), the line spacing is tighter, and the punter lines up closer to the line of scrimmage, kicking from a "pocket."

Figure 8–3. *The tight punt formation.*

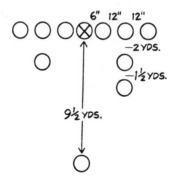

On the tight punt, linemen have to hold their blocks longer and then cover the kick. (See Figure 8–4.)

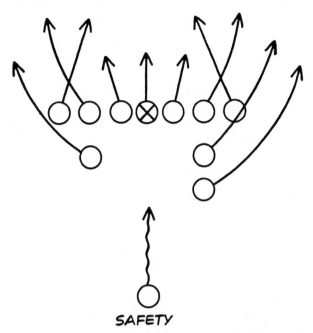

SAFETY

Figure 8–4. *Punt coverage from the tight punt formation.*

Coaching points concerning the tight punt are the following:

(1) Never use the tight punt unless you are back of your own 3 yard line.

(2) Reduce splits.

(3) Hold block and sprint on the thump of the ball. Ends can leave early.

(4) The punting team must sprint hard for wide coverage because they have reduced their splits which tends to group the team together.

(5) The up backs and the deep back should never move their inside foot out of position.

(6) Interior linemen have the following blocking: block inside gap —if no one is in the gap they should block the man over them.

(7) Right end can forearm block as he releases and sprints hard. He must keep the punt receiver to the inside.

(8) Left end—holds the block for one count and then sprints hard
    —contains the safety.
(9) Kicker—with blocks being held longer, he should try to look
    at the ball and get a good kick. He covers as a safety man.

The Quick Kick

To have a good, balanced attack every team should employ a quick
kick. There are several different formations a team can line up in when
using the quick kick. Primarily, it depends on which back you are using
as your kicker. We have used our tailbacks and fullbacks. It is an ideal
play if the fullback has the ability to kick the ball, because the center
has a straight look in snapping the ball to him. Usually if the tailback is
the kicker, it is necessary to cheat him over a little. Let me stress strongly
that the formation should resemble a running or passing formation because it is necessary that the play be a complete surprise for it to be
effective. It is necessary to hold the defensive secondary in tight to give
the ball a chance to hit the ground and roll in an effective manner.

Our protection and coverage is exactly the same as that for our tight
punt; our slotback assumes the duties of the right end. We seal block to
the inside with the slotback. Our fullback moves forward quickly to protect on the strong side. The quarterback should place his hands under
the center to resemble a running play. The quarterback widens his feet
to give the center more room, and protects on the weak side. The kicker
cheats back as deep as possible without giving the play away. The center
passes the ball through the quarterback's legs directly at the kicker's
right knee. This will permit the kicker to stay in a low, crouched position. The kicker should kick an end-over-end type kick, which may get
very good roll.

The ends', tackles', and guards' rule is to block the inside gap. If no
one is in this gap, then they block the man over them.

The center blocks the man in the gap to the offside. If no one is
there he blocks the man over him. (See Figure 8–5.)

Some basic coaching points relative to the quick kick are the following:

(1) Make the play resemble a running play but be careful not to
    give it away.
(2) Cheat the backs deeper. The ideal depth is 5 yards.
(3) The quarterback should widen the base of his legs.

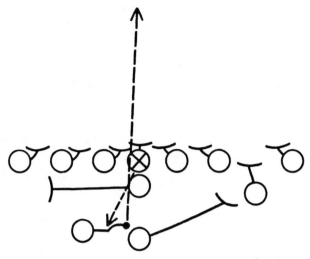

Figure 8–5. *The quick kick from the tight slot formation.*

(4) The center should put his head down at the last possible second and make a perfect snap.

(5) The kicker should stay in a crouched position and he should meet the ball with such a kick that it will produce an end-over-end kick.

(6) The fullback must move up toward the line quickly for the blocking assignment. He should never give ground and he must stay low.

(7) Each lineman should be cautioned to block low and to his inside.

(8) After the ball has been kicked, all of the men should spread out in order to cover the kick.

The Punt Return

Punt returns have broken up many football games. To be effective on the punt return, it is necessary to have a good punt returner. He should have good speed, agility, toughness, and he must be able to perform with a cool head.

We use a couple of punt return patterns in our attack so that we will not always look the same when we are putting on a punt return. (See Figure 8–6.)

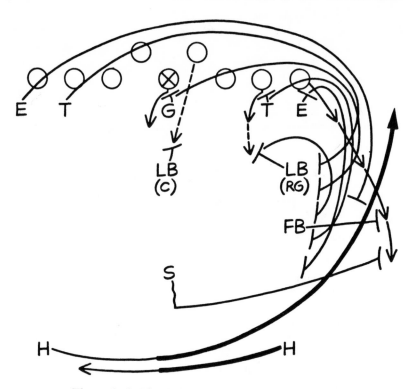

Figure 8–6. *The 5–3–1–2 punt return vs. the 7–2 spread punt.*

The rules and assignments for the five-man punt return are the following:

RIGHT END: Holds up end and turns back downfield blocking into ball.

RIGHT TACKLE: Holds up tackle and turns back to form a wall.

LEFT GUARD: Holds up center and turns back to form a wall.

LEFT TACKLE: Drives through tackle, forces punter, and turns back to form wall.

LEFT END: Rushes outside end and makes punter kick. Sprints behind wall and cleans up.

RIGHT GUARD: Lines up 6 yards behind end and throws cross body block on the first man to show inside. Then rolls back to form inside wall on pursuing opponents.

CENTER: Lines up 6 yards behind guard and throws cross body
block on first man to show inside. Then rolls back to form inside
wall on pursuing opponents.

FULLBACK: Lines up 8 to 10 yards behind end and goes across field
blocking end out on side of return.

SAFETY: Protects halfbacks by locking first man down. Fair catches
short, high punts.

HALFBACKS: Fields punts and returns to the side called. Man without ball carries out good fake.

Another punt return alignment that is much like the five-man front
return that we use utilizes only a single safety man. But, on this return,
the defensive halfbacks are in a position to handle short kicks. (See
Figure 8–7.)

Figure 8–7. *The 7–1–2–1 punt return vs. the 7–2
spread punt.*

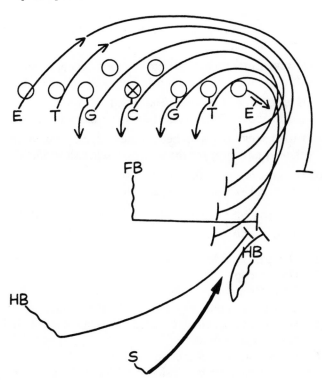

The rules and assignments for the seven-man punt return are the following:

RIGHT END: Lines up on the first man on the line of scrimmage. Forces him outside. Turns and goes to meet the safety, blocking the first man to show.

RIGHT TACKLE: Lines up on the second man on the line of scrimmage, forces him inside, turns and sets wall about 25 yards.

RIGHT GUARD: Lines up on the third man on the line of scrimmage. (Might line up on up back by scout report.) Forces him away from the side of return and forms wall behind tackle.

CENTER: Lines up on the center, forces him away from the side of return, and forms wall behind guard.

LEFT GUARD: Lines up on third man on line of scrimmage (might line up on up back by scout report), and forces him away from the side of return. Forms wall behind center.

LEFT TACKLE: Blocks the punt, if he misses he forms wall behind guard.

LEFT END: Blocks the punt. If he misses, he is the cleanup man behind the wall.

FULLBACK: Lines up behind center 7 yards deep. Blocks end out on side of return. (Alignment may vary and timing is all important.)

RIGHT HALFBACK: Lines up behind end, 25 yards deep. Blocks first man to show. Catches short kicks to the side or in the middle.

LEFT HALFBACK: Lines up behind the end, 35 yards deep. He is the personal interferer for the safety. Catches short kicks to the side.

SAFETY: Lines up in the middle 40–45 yards deep. Starts up the middle and wheels out to get behind the wall.

Some basic coaching points to follow while teaching the punt return to your players are these:

(1) Don't be offside.
(2) Do not clip.
(3) Do not rough the kicker.
(4) The safety should catch all punts, if possible.
(5) Use a verbal sound to warn unseeing players that the ball has hit the ground.
(6) Do not block near a bouncing ball.
(7) Do not field the ball inside the 10 yard line.
(8) Have confidence in the punt return.

The Punt Rush

The punt rush is a very good weapon to use in wet, cold weather when there is more likelihood of a mishandled snap from center.

The punt rush also serves as a holdup type of defense because the punting team has to tighten up its alignment and block longer; therefore, they are slower in releasing to cover the kick.

We use the corner rush and the middle rush in order to block punts. (See Figures 8–8 and 8–9.)

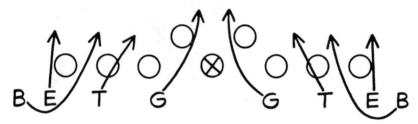

Figure 8–8. *The corner punt rush vs. the 7–2 spread punt.*

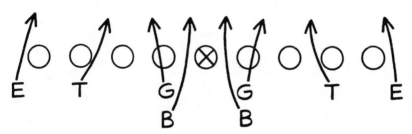

Figure 8–9. *The middle rush vs. the nine-man spread punt.*

The Kickoff Return

The kickoff return is a vital play in the football game. Every effort should be made to get the ball out to the 30 yard line on every kickoff. The chances of driving the ball over 70 yards, without a penalty or other error, are slim.

We use two kickoff returns and both of them have proved successful. (See Figures 8–10 and 8–11.) One is a sideline return and the other is a middle return.

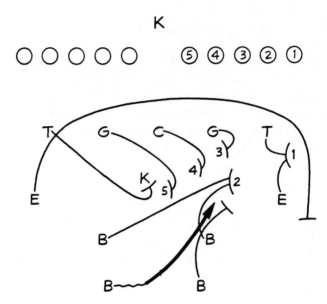

Figure 8–10. *The sideline kickoff return.*

Figure 8–11. *The middle return (wedge).*

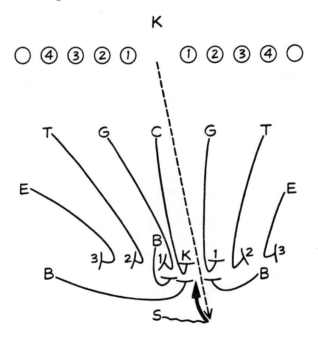

On the wedge return, the center should turn and sprint in the direction of the flight of the ball. The other linemen sprint and converge upon the center. At a point 10 to 15 yards from the ballcarrier, the center turns around and blocks the kicker. The left guard blocks the #1 man to the left of the kicker, and the right guard blocks the #1 man to the right of the kicker. The other linemen block their respective assignments.

The Anti-Onside Kickoff Return

There are times in football games when a team receiving a kickoff knows that the kicking team is going to try an onside kick. In such situations, every precaution should be made to insure against a successful onside kick.

We use a certain alignment (See Figure 8–12) in this situation. We want quick, agile, aggressive people in the recovery positions. Our plan is to bring the linemen up to the 49 yard line and to bring three special substitutes up to the 43 yard line. If the ball is kicked through the linemen they block in front of the ball. If the ball looks as if it might not get on through, the linemen recover the ball.

Figure 8–12. *The anti-onside kickoff return.*

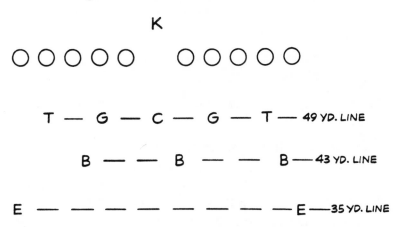

The Extra Point and Field Goal

The field goal and the extra point are vital parts of the kicking game. The field goal affords a team the opportunity to score from within 10 to 50 yards of the opposition's goal.

The linemen protecting for the extra points and field goals should be as big as possible in order to widen the corners and present insurmountable obstacles for the defense to get by.

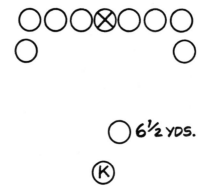

Figure 8–13. *The extra point and field goal alignment.*

The rules and assignments for the extra point and field goal are as follows:

CENTER: Good snap, raises up and blocks big.

GUARDS: Lines up elbows on knees in two point stances with no split between guard and center. On the snap, brings arms up and protects the inside gap, stays square and is big.

TACKLES AND ENDS: Splits 3 inches, the rest of the technique is like guards.

SLOTBACK: Lines up in two-point stance with inside foot splitting end's feet. On snap braces up, protects inside first.

$\mathbf{A}$ction is the beginning of everything. In football, as in every other human activity, nothing of any consequence happens until an individual or a team wants to act. What is accomplished depends to a large extent on how much, and why, one wants to act. Thus, the basic aim of a football coach should be to motivate into action a team that will utilize every talent it has available, on as many given occasions as possible. Everything that is done, every thought that is considered, should be designed along the lines of utilizing in the individual player, and then in the team as a whole, every bit of talent that is available. If the resource or talent is reasonably good and properly motivated to act, then a basis of winning football is established.

This basic aim of utilizing the team's talent through motivation to action can be accomplished by acquiring what may loosely be called emotional maturity, and emotional unity. Emotional maturity

9

Establishing the Winning Emotion for the Ball-Control Game

may be defined as a positive attitude coupled with competence that is brought about by proper training on the practice field. The object of emotional maturity is to produce a well-trained football team that is fundamentally sound in all facets of the game. Emotional maturity, then, is the technical training of the football team, and was the basis for discussion in the previous eight chapters of this book. Emotional unity, on the other hand, is the basic philosophy aimed at motivating the football player.

Emotional Unity

The objective of emotional unity is to strive to create among players and coaches a deep feeling of togetherness in their efforts toward the common goal of winning. This same comrade feeling should exist among all elements that are involved in the program in one way or another. Then, as one strives to unify his players and coaches to a common goal, he should also make an effort to encourage athletic department officials, school officials, faculty, students, and booster groups to feel like a part of the team. In order for this *esprit de corps* to prevail, a set philosophy compatible with good human relationship must be established and maintained with all of the facets that make up the program. The football coach has a great responsibility to each group that has an interest in his program, and a discussion of each of these in light of attaining the desired *esprit de corps* is appropriate.

The Administration

It is important to have a president or a principal who understands the program and is anxious to support it. The best way the administration can initiate help is to give the coach a good contract. The contract is important mainly as a means of assuring the coach that his program will have an opportunity to be built on a solid foundation. It usually takes four or five years to shape a ball club into winning form. Without the security of a long-term contract a coach may find himself compromising on sound principles in an effort to produce an immediate winner. For example, the coach may find himself playing individuals of questionable character in an effort to win immediately, instead of concentrating on solid citizens who in the long run will beget a sounder, winning program. A planned program that has the assurance of time will have a better chance of being built on a broad and solid foundation.

While it is vitally important to have an administration that wants to help and support the program, the coach has a grave responsibility to justify that support. This can be accomplished by a basic understanding on his part that he works for and represents an educational institution, and that all of his actions reflect directly upon the administration and the educational system. The coach should keep uppermost in his mind that his function as a part of the institution is to educate students through participation in the game of football. He should constantly make an effort to inspire his players to achieve academic success, as well as football success, so that through the educational values learned in both, the student-athlete will be better prepared for his life ahead. The coach should also be thoroughly aware of the administration's policies, rules, and regulations, and be willing to give whole-hearted support to them. In the event that differences of opinion develop over an activated policy, they should be discussed behind closed doors and not aired publicly. Once a decision is made, however, the coach, of course, is responsible for supporting the policy.

The coach also has an obligation to keep his president informed of what he is doing or attempting to do in any significant situation. On the other side of the ledger, the president should also strive to keep his coach informed on issues relative to his job. As long as there is this constant flow of information, one to the other, there is established a mutual understanding which is necessary for the coach to gain the administrative support needed. This type of relationship with the administration will virtually assure the coach that almost any reasonable request will be granted where possible.

The Athletic Director

If the football coach is not the athletic director, it is important that the man in charge of the athletic department be an asset and contribute to the football program. It is best, of course, to have as the director of athletics one who has coached football, and therefore has a thorough understanding of the problems of the game. An experienced and well-organized athletic director can offer sound advice to the football coach, but of course he must be careful not to interfere directly and consequently handicap the coach in his responsibility of directing his team. On such matters as scheduling, team travel, academic problems, awards program, etc., a good athletic director can contribute a great deal to the program.

It is vitally important that a harmonious relationship exist between the coach and the athletic director. Because of the close contact required in the two jobs, it is helpful if the coach and the athletic director have adjoining offices. Almost daily contact on matters is important in order that an atmosphere of mutual respect and understanding prevails. The coach, of course, should have the right and privilege to suggest and initiate any action which has to do with the conduct or improvement of the football program. Where differences of opinion exist on controversial matters, they should be discussed behind closed doors and in a friendly manner. Once, however, a final decision is reached it should be accepted and given complete support by the coach.

The Faculty

A cordial relationship between the athletic department and the faculty is extremely important to the success of the football program. By the coach projecting a wholesome image of his program, he stands a good chance of maintaining a fine working relationship with the faculty. Generally, most faculty members are as interested as the coach in seeing that their school is well represented. The coach, however, through his program, must justify the support of the faculty.

The football program's goal should be to produce the best and most efficient department on campus. This, of course, should be the objective of every school department from History through Physics. However, while the coach strives to make his department the best, he should never lose sight of the fact that his is only one of the many departments that go to make up the total school. At all times, the football program should be kept in that perspective.

Faculty interest in the football program is derived from a basic understanding of the aims of the department. This can best be accomplished by the coach making a genuine effort to try and understand what the individual faculty member hopes to accomplish in his particular department. Occasional visits by the coach to the various departments to learn more about their function and to understand their problems will certainly stimulate mutual interest. By taking the opportunity to talk and share ideas with faculty members at lunch and at various school functions, the coach can help promote friendship and understanding. Good spirit on the part of the faculty toward the football program will pay lasting dividends.

The Student Body

Student body support is an absolute must for a successful football program. Enthusiastic spirit by the students at football games is oftentimes the winning edge. In almost all cases, the so-called home field advantage that a team enjoys is the inspirational support given by the students during the game. If that support is forthcoming, it must be justified.

To gain the support of students, each football player must be respected both on and off the field. He must be willing during the game to give an all-out effort for school victory. He must also be willing during school to assume his responsibilities as a student and, whenever possible, to integrate in various school activities. No individual in school is respected more than the football player who during the game competes with the best, but during the week takes a vital part in school activities, and still maintains good grades. More often than not, the most respected community leaders come from this type of individual. Not all football players are blessed with the talent of having such balanced leadership qualities, but certainly every athlete can be a respected citizen in school. A football team must be composed of this type student-athlete if the necessary support is to be forthcoming.

Besides reminding his football players of their responsibilities as both students and athletes, the coach and his staff can be a direct help in gaining student support. A coach should not pass up an opportunity whenever possible to speak to student groups. The students appreciate the opportunity of knowing their coach better, and this in turn affords him the opportunity to promote his program. Such things as the importance of school spirit to a football team and the pride that should be taken in that spirit can be pointed out. In addition, a coach should, whenever possible, take an active part in school activities. Students who notice the coach's interest in their projects are forever grateful to him. By identifying directly with the students, the coach has greatly enhanced the possibilities of maintaining vital school spirit.

Booster Groups

Booster organizations that are properly controlled can be a tremendous asset to the football program. Both their financial and moral support is needed for a successful operation. However, such groups must be utilized within the framework of institutional controls. A coach should never attempt to use such groups to further his program in a way that is not in keeping with existing rules and regulations. Booster groups should never be allowed to establish a position of influence concerning the operation of a football team. Strong leadership, both by the school administration and the coach, will keep the influence of the booster group in its proper perspective.

While the coach should take an active part in the development of the booster club, he should leave room for initiative within the organization. The club basically should be composed of a president, vice-president, secretary-treasurer, and a board of directors. Annual rotation of all positions with the possible exception of secretary-treasurer is desirable in order to stimulate interest among a good cross-section of people within the community. Each administration should be allowed to develop its organization and program, as long as it is compatible with the coach's objectives. Annual sponsorship of the football banquet and recognition of achievement through awards are standard, worthy projects for the club. In addition, variable yearly projects should be initiated, in view of the football team's current needs.

The coach plays the primary role in the development of enthusiasm which is needed for the success of the club. The only reason for the club's existence is to support the program, and consequently, the coach has the responsibility to keep it alive. He should constantly strive to make the booster club meetings as interesting as possible. Diagrams of important plays, films of the ball games, and discussion of individual players are always interesting to the club. The coach should, throughout his association with the boosters, attempt to develop the necessary pride and loyalty in the organization and the team. An active, well-controlled booster club is a vital cog in the football wheel.

News Media

It is extremely important that the coach has a good working relationship with the various members of the news media. Favorable news releases are an asset to the program by creating player, parent, and fan interest, and by selling tickets to the games. Furthermore, the coach, in order to be completely successful, must communicate with the public. The best method of doing this is through newspapers, radio, and television. The coach must first, however, develop a positive attitude in his news relations and be aware of his responsibilities to the news media if he is to expect the desired results.

A sound attitude for the coach to develop is to first try and understand that the news media have a job and a responsibility to report the news to the public. This responsibility of reporting information is one of the basic freedoms of our democratic system. It is up to the coach, then, to develop a program that will be reported on in a favorable manner. A good guideline to follow in dealing with the news media is to be honest, courteous, cooperative, and fair. Statements that are derogatory and misleading should be avoided, and whenever direct questions are asked, they should be answered honestly and in a straightforward manner. Dissemination of news should be evenly divided between morning and afternoon releases, but a reporter who comes to the coach with an idea for a story should have the privilege of an exclusive.

It is important that a coach reaches the public to keep it informed of his players and the team. Most college coaches are fortunate to have a sports information director on the regular staff. Those coaches who do not have such a staff member should find someone interested in sports to keep the news media informed. A sports information director is a valuable asset to the program and a harmonious association with him is important. He should be permitted to operate on his own initiative and authority, and a good, imaginative one will make a special contribution to team morale. The proper selection of news stories by the sports information director on both the team and the individual player can boost, tremendously, the morale of those concerned. It is a good policy for the sports information director to interview each player on the team so that a story is written about him in light of his special contribution to team success. This is true of every player, regardless of whether he is a member of the starting team or not. It is doubtful that favorable publicity will win any football games, but it can have a direct effect on the team and it is a most important part of the coach's job.

The Coaching Staff and the Team

While it is important that a good *esprit de corps* exist among the various components that are concerned with the football program, their part in the actual success of the plan is insignificant when compared to the assistant coaches and the players. A head football coach literally sinks or swims with his assistants and his players. Very simply stated, the assistants do the coaching and the athletes do the playing, and therein the games are won or lost. The head coach who is able to surround himself with a dedicated staff of hard-working coaches and a devoted group of talented athletes will produce a winner. His main concern then will be to strive to maintain among his coaches and players a deep feeling of comradeship in their efforts toward the common goal of winning. If this spirit is to prevail, a set philosophy compatible with good human relations is of vital importance to the head coach.

The Assistant Coaches

Perhaps the biggest decision that a head coach has to make involves choosing his coaching staff. The complete success of his plan depends upon the head coach surrounding himself with a knowledgeable group of loyal, dedicated, hard-working assistants who want to sacrifice and cooperate for the goal of a winning program. The decision is so important that a great deal of patience should be exercised in trying to hire the right men. He should examine carefully the prospective coaches' qualifications before making a job offer.

An assistant coach must be so dedicated to the game of football that he wants to work as much as is necessary to win. This requires spending long hours of detailed and concentrated work which takes him away from his family relaxation and prevents a normal routine. Coaching is not a routine clock-punching job, and the person who does not want to make the necessary sacrifice should not be in the coaching profession. The head coach cannot expect his staff to be dedicated to their work unless he sets the proper example. If he expects to have a dedicated, hard-working staff, he must work harder and longer than his assistants.

Loyalty to the head coach and his program is another valuable quality that the assistant must possess. However, loyalty is a two-way street and begins with the head coach. He must at all times be honest and straightforward with his staff, and treat them with proper respect. Once a coach hires a staff, he should have complete confidence in it and be convinced that his staff is the best in the country. Only by this type of attitude can the head coach expect and receive the type of loyalty that his assistants must give to him and his program.

The assistant coach must also possess a sound understanding of the game of football and be willing, at every opportunity, to improve his knowledge. The assistant coach must constantly search for more and better ways to teach the game. Attendance at coaching clinics, visitations with other coaches, and detailed film study are some of the many ways a coach can improve his knowledge of the game. Encouragement by the head coach for the staff to take advantage of these opportunities certainly is desirable.

The ability to get along with other people and understand human nature is another basic requirement for an assistant coach. Though this quality is best attained and nurtured through experience, some coaches seem to be naturally gifted with this ability. The quality of getting along with his players and fellow coaches affords a coach the best opportunity for getting maximum results from his coaching. Most boys are different, and while they should all be treated alike, the coach who possesses the quality of understanding individual appeals likely will get maximum performance. Likewise, a coaching staff is made up of many different individuals, and the assistant must be willing to understand his fellow coaches and work in harmony for the program. Occasional staff meetings by the head coach for the purpose of discussing human nature, and the importance of staff cooperation, are worthwhile.

Coaching Is Teaching

Once the coach is hired, he must be allowed to exploit his talents in his job specification. He should be allowed to coach on the field, and the head coach should never attempt to take the initiative away from him by interfering with his group instruction. A coach is first and foremost a teacher, and he must constantly strive to improve his teaching techniques. The type of coaching job he does depends solely upon his ability to pass on his personal knowledge of the game to his players. What he knows is of little value unless he can teach it to the ones who play the game. The attitude of the head coach and his staff should be that the only way to do a good coaching job is to do a good teaching job, regardless of the pupils available. It is a poor coach who would blame unprepared athletes for mistakes in a game. To get the maximum out of coaching, the only attitude a staff should take for a boy's shortcomings in a game is that, "I did a poor coaching job on him."

The Staff Advises

One of the primary functions of the assistant coach is to advise his head coach. With the varied responsibilities the head coach assumes, he is constantly dependent upon the advice of his staff. The head coach should not only seek his staff's advice, but welcome their informed convictions on matters—even though, at times, their proposals are contrary to his expressed opinions. An assistant who is a so-called "yes" man makes little contribution to the head coach. However, once the head coach makes a decision, and even though it is contrary to the expressed beliefs of a staff member, the assistant is expected to carry out that decision in an enthusiastic manner. This type of loyalty is expected of the staff, and any member who falls short of his responsibilities will have a poor professional career. Likewise, the head coach who is not loyal to his assistants, nor listens to their advice and opinion, is committing professional suicide. The head coach and his staff must work in an atmosphere of mutual respect and loyalty if the program is to succeed.

Delegate Authority, Not Responsibility

A football team without good squad morale will never reach its potential as a team. Good squad morale is radiated from good staff morale. Therefore, it should be a vital concern of the head coach to see that the morale of his staff is constantly at or near peak level. Delegation of authority over particular phases of the game is one motivating factor for good morale. By the head coach delegating authority, the assistant enjoys a vital position of influence and is contributing directly to the program. An assistant coach who does indeed feel that he has an important job to perform will become "ego involved" in his work. He will naturally strive for excellence through personal pride in his job. His enthusiasm will be at a maximum level, which will, of course, be contagious to those around him. By a coach having authority over a specialized phase of the game, maximum results will be assured—from both player and coach.

The head coach must realize that while he delegates authority to his assistants he cannot delegate responsibility in the true sense of the word. He alone is responsible for the performance of his team, and he must be mentally conditioned to publicly accept the blame if the team plays poorly. At the same time, a head coach should quickly praise the staff members both privately and publicly for a good performance by the ball club. Only when a team performs well should the head coach delegate job responsibility.

Good staff morale is an outgrowth of many things. Respectable pay and fringe benefits, along with good working facilities, are beneficial to good morale. The feeling of basic security, as best as it can be offered in the coaching profession, is a help to staff morale. However, besides the more materialistic benefits a staff member enjoys, he must feel the more intangible human rewards that come from good working conditions. A staff member should be treated with respect and dealt with fairly. He should participate in the management of affairs and be consulted instead of constantly directed on matters. He should be given a position of importance and influence so that he may experience the personal satisfaction of a job well done. The head coach has a responsibility to treat his staff with an attitude of good human relations if he intends to maintain good staff morale. If the morale of his coaching staff is high, it will permeate the football team.

The Player and the Team

Be Yourself

The last and certainly the most important consideration of all is the football team. To be sure, when the whistle sounds at game time, ultimate victory or defeat rests entirely upon the performance of the team. In turn, how they perform is the sole responsibility of the coach. Thus, the basic aim of football coaching should be to motivate into action a team that will utilize as much talent as it has available on as many given occasions as possible. There is no one, proven, absolute method of accomplishing this end. There have been numerous examples of successful coaches, each with his own individual style. While some of these coaches adhered to similar basic principles of coaching, their methods ranged from one extreme to another. The classical example has been the apparent contrasting coaching philosophies of Bobby Dodd of Georgia Tech and Paul Bryant of Alabama . . . both, however, extremely successful coaches. If there was any one common denominator that was used by all of the successful coaches, it was that all of them coached their teams according to their own personalities. True, many of them borrowed ideas and emulated other coaches to a certain extent, but in the application of those methods and theories, they did so without altering their own style and personality. Many a coach has failed trying to carbon-copy another coach's methods. Thus, the wise head coach learns from others, *yet adopts those ideas to his own style.* This point should be kept in mind during the discussion of the football player.

Player Evaluation

Everyone connected with football knows that quality personnel is the key to success. The team that is faster, bigger, stronger, and more dedicated normally will win in a contest. However, since no one has a continued monopoly on superior talent, personnel must be properly evaluated and utilized in an attempt to get maximum results from the material one has available. For instance, it would logically be foolish for a coach to take a passing quarterback who is not a good runner, and try to employ the split-T and outside belly series which calls for a good running quarterback. Likewise, it would be foolish to run a "pro-passing" attack with a quarterback who is not a naturally gifted passer. Defensively, it would be unwise for a coach to major in a "straight defense" without stunting if his line is quick but very small. These are simple examples of not properly utilizing available material. The coach should constantly analyze the talent of every boy and try to adopt a style of play that will bring out the best of his physical abilities.

Play Performance

While there are many athletes with fine physical abilities, all of them are not what we call football players. On the other hand, there are many athletes who are less talented than others, but by utilization of their talents through hard work and dedication, they become good football players. It is the coach's job to properly evaluate his personnel so that he is playing the boy who performs instead of the boy who has the potential to perform. While a coach should never give up on potential (for one day it may develop), he should play only the one who performs the best—regardless of his size, speed, or other natural talents. The simplest and best way for a coach to assure himself that he is playing the best boy is to grade the performance of each boy on each play.

This assures the coach that he is playing the boy who performs instead of the boy who may have only the potential to perform.

The Type of Player

A well-known coach was once quoted as saying that every coach should look for the boy who will "rise above the coaching." This type of player is the one who comes along occasionally and is gifted with superior talent and motivation. He is the one who time after time makes the winning play in ball games . . . the play that has never been taught by his coach. There are not too many of these type players around, and fortunate is the coach who has had the privilege of coaching a few of them.

While there are a limited number of players who "rise above the coaching," there are quite a few boys who possess the qualities of a winner. The winning football player must possess certain character traits in addition to basic physical talent. He must be dedicated to football to the extent that he is willing to work, sacrifice, and cooperate for team victory. He must be personally ambitious enough to want to excel to his maximum. He must be tough both physically and mentally, which will enable him to fight to the end despite the odds against him. He must possess and work to develop qualities of leadership both on and off the field. Finally, he must be willing to subordinate himself at all times for the glory of the team. A coach who is blessed with players who possess these character traits will have a winner even, at times, in spite of himself.

Morale

Morale, defined, is a "great aggressive spirit of whole-hearted co-operation in a common effort." This emotional feeling of unity in the effort toward the common goal of winning must be present if a team is to realize its potential. If the head coach has a staff whose morale is high, he has solved the greatest portion of team morale problems. To be sure, good staff morale radiates and permeates into good team morale. A coaching staff that is united and spirited will produce a team that is united and spirited. The same general principles that were previously discussed as paramount to staff morale are also applicable in many ways to team morale. There are, in addition, further points of importance that are worthy of discussion. What type of relationship should exist between coach and player? What is the attitude of the coach in developing and sustaining the all-important element of pride in his team?

Coach-Player Relationship

It is absolutely important that mutual respect be established and maintained between coach and player. The best way to start is for the coach to adopt the attitude that he will treat his players in the same manner that he was or wanted to be treated when he was a player. If this attitude prevails, almost all coaches will strive to maintain the dignity of the athlete both as an individual and as a human being.

Oftentimes coaches forget the tremendous influence they can exert on their football players. Perhaps of all the responsible positions in our country, there is no group that has a greater influence on people than the coach. Particularly is this true of the high school coach who deals so directly with his players during the formative ages of their lives. So often the coach can tip the scales on the right side for a boy during this critical time. Thus, it is the responsibility of the coach to realize his position and exert the proper influence on his players.

The coach should encourage his players as students as well as athletes. He should stand ready and even encourage his players to come to him for help and advice with their personal problems. He should discuss with them lessons of values that are important to football as well as to life. One of the great rewards of coaching is the association with many boys, and the opportunity to be able to help them in some way. It is very satisfying to a coach to see a boy he coached do well in life. The coach experiences a wonderful feeling when he thinks that in some small way he helped prepare the boy for his chosen vocation.

There are some very basic, commonsense guidelines that a coach should follow in dealing with his players on the field. While it is wise for him to study other coaches to increase his knowledge and teaching ability, he should coach according to his own personality. A coach who carbon copies another coach's methods cannot be effective, for he will eventually portray an image of insincerity to his players. The coach should further avoid the danger of letting his personal dislikes influence his judgment of his players. Football is perhaps the most democratic institution in America today; a coach should never allow personal prejudices to enter into his judgment. If a coach makes a commitment to his players, he must stand ready to back his promise. If he tells his squad they will practice only an hour on a particular day, under no circumstances should they practice longer. Likewise, a coach who threatens punishment should be sure that it is administered. Much respect is lost for a coach who does not back his threats with action. It is wise for the coach to keep his players informed of why certain things are done. They tend to perform better when they know the purpose of certain drills, etc., that they may be called upon to do. Although basically all players should be treated alike, a coach should remember that all players are different. The coach should always strive to find the type of appeal that will bring out the best in a particular boy.

In order for the coach to maintain the proper discipline needed, he must maintain that delicate balance between closeness and familiarity. He must be close enough to properly direct maximum performance, but yet not so close that he will lose control. It has often been said that a maestro conducting an orchestra is in the right position to maintain the proper balance of control. The coach who assumes such a position can properly control his discipline policy. Perhaps the best policy or discipline is to be "fair but firm." It is good to have as few rules as possible, so as not to burden the players with unnecessary restrictions. However, the rules that are set forth should be strictly enforced.

Every coach has to deal with the boy who makes a serious mistake. Without exception, the boy who violates a rule must be disciplined immediately. There should be no compromise in this respect. However, every boy should be given an opportunity for a second chance provided, of course, that he really wants it and is willing to sacrifice for it. The coach who has been willing to help a boy help himself under such conditions has been rewarded more often than not. The right type of boy will take advantage of his opportunity and become an even better performer. If he is not the right type of boy, he will err seriously again, and then there should no longer be a place for him on the team.

Pride

There has never been a success story in football or any other endeavor without pride being the keynote. The finding and developing of pride in a boy is a complex endeavor. In most cases, reasonable pride in one's possessions coupled with a proper amount of humility is a character trait that some boys have acquired naturally. In most cases, however, this pride must be sustained and developed. A winning tradition is a great pride-builder, but on the other hand, it is impossible to have a winning tradition without pride. As complex as the subject is, the coach should constantly search for the boys with built-in pride, and then strive to develop and sustain it.

There are some special individuals who have been endowed with what we may call rare pride. They are the athletes who are referred to as those who "rise above the coaching." These boys, regardless of the environment that surrounds them, will work to do the best they possibly can. They could be playing on the worst football team in America, and be coached by the worst coach, but they still would give maximum performance. These types of players are, of course, the rare exception. The pride of almost all other players must be nurtured and sustained. It is the coach's job to help them find and feel a reason to be proud.

If the coach has pride in his job, the team is more apt to develop it. He should personally take great pride in the school he represents and encourage his players to feel the same way. He should work to make his program the very best. Within the limits of a reasonable budget, the coach should strive to provide his players with facilities of which they can be proud. Well-cared-for equipment, practice and playing fields, training and locker rooms, and neatly kept offices all can provide a team with a feeling of pride. This is especially true if in some way the players themselves contributed toward maintaining the facilities. If the coach provides first-class facilities for his players, he is in more of a position to demand first-class performance.

Pride can further be developed by the coach if he helps his players establish a set of values that is important in football, as well as life in general. Short lectures by the coach on such important values as teamwork, loyalty, dedication, sacrifice, and many others are important to the development of the boys' winning character. Not only are these character traits important to winning football, but also they are important to winning citizenship. The coach who constantly impresses the importance of these types of principles upon his players is taking a big step in pride building.

Development of senior leadership among squad members is the last important pride-builder. To be sure, a good team is always characterized by good senior leadership. The coach should encourage his experienced, more mature players to assume this vital leadership role. The seniors who enjoy a sense of special importance and influence on the team are more personally involved and consequently more apt to strive for better performance. Discussions of the principles of leadership by the coach with his seniors is helpful in developing the desired results. Seeking the seniors' advice on certain matters is helpful in developing in them a feeling of special participation concerning team decisions. The senior should be afforded special privileges. This not only develops leadership, but also helps the younger players aspire to work for the rewards of being a senior. The naming of senior game captains, the granting of special senior awards, and the limiting of practice time for seniors are just a few of the special privileges that can be granted to them. The development of pride by the seniors will permeate the rest of the team. The team that is proud will not be beaten easily.

Index

A

Advice to head coach one of assistant coach's main functions, 210
Administration, role of in building emotional unity, 202–203
Alabama, 211
Alignment of offensive backs, 48–49
All pass drill for receiving by offensive end, 129–130
Anti-onside kickoff return, 199
Aprons, use of in practice, 43
Assistant coaches, role of, 208–209
Athletic director, role of in establishing emotional unity, 203–204
Authority, delegation of by head coach, 210–211

B

Backs, offensive, coaching, 45–64
  alignment, 48–49
  blocking, 54–57
    drills, 61–63
  center and quarterback exchange, 50–51

Backs (contd.)
    drill, 63–64
  drills, 57–61
    (see also "Drills for offensive backs")
  fumble recovery drill, 63
  moving on snap of ball, 50
  points, essential, 57
  quarterback techniques and ball handling, 51–54
  stance, 46–48
Bad pass drill for receiving by offensive ends, 131–132
Ballcarriers, offensive ends as, 137
"Baylor" concept of throwing, 32
"Bend-in" route as pass route for offensive ends, 135
Blocking by backs, 54–57
  cut block, 55
  pass protection block, 56
  post drive, 55
  power block, 54–55
  running shoulder block, 56
Blocking stunts, 88–118
  even defenses, 103–118
  odd defenses, 88–103

221

Blocks for offensive ends, types of, 124–126
  double team, 124–125
  downfield, 125–126
  drive block, 124
  peelback, 126
  reverse shoulder block, 124
Board drill, 62
  for offensive ends, 127
  using man with aprons, 74
  with dummies, 73–74
Body balance drill, 58–59
Body control drill, 58
Booster groups, importance of to success of football program, 206
"Bootleg," definition of, 143–144
Bootleg protection of pass, 83–85
Bootleg technique for quarterbacks, 52
Bryant, Paul, 211
Butt as technique of offensive end, 129

C

Center and quarterback exchange, 50–51
  drill, 63–64
Center most important person in kicking game, 189–190
Center's stance, 69
Checklist, practice, of fundamentals and techniques for offensive linemen, 28–29
Chute drill, 60–61
Circle hook route as pass route for offensive ends, 133–134
Coach-player relationship, 214–215
Concentration drill for receiving by offensive ends, 131
Consistency of every player important for winning team, 2
Counter trap of inside belly series, 20
"Cross" in line call, 119–120
Crowther sled drills for offensive ends, 126–127
Cut block, 55, 152
Cutoff block, 79–80
  drill, 80

D

Defenses most widely used in Georgia running game, 4–9

Delay route as pass route for offensive ends, 137
Desire to win important for winning team, 2
Diversified sets in running game, 24–26
Dodd, Bobby, 211
"Double" in line call, 119
Double team blocking, 81–82
  by offensive ends, 124–125
Downfield blocking, 82
  by offensive ends, 125–126
Drills, blocking, 61–62
  board drill, 62
  punching drill, 61–62
  technique drills, 62
Drills, blocking, for offensive ends, 126–127
Drills for offensive backfield, 57–61
  body balance, 58–59
  body control, 58
  chute drill, 60–61
  obstacle course drill, 59–60
  spin, 58
  staggered bag obstacle course, 60
  stiff-arm drill, 57
Drive block, 71–75
  by offensive ends, 124
  drills, 72–75
Drop-back pass, 139
Drop-stepping as technique for bootleg protection, 83–84
Dummy situation in practice, 43

E

Effort important for winning team, 1–2
"Ego involvement" of assistant coaches encouraged by head coach's delegation of authority, 210–211
Eight man front defenses and possible stunting combinations, 103–118
Elements, three, of passing attack, 140–141
Emotion, establishing winning, 201–217
  administration, 202–203
  athletic director, 203–204
  booster groups, 206
  coaching staff and team, 207–211
  advice, 210